Graham Cray has long been known as a perceptive watcher of culture. In this important and accessible book, he skilfully weaves together social science, biblical analysis and prophetic wisdom in offering a much-needed vision of public discipleship: the vital role churches can and do play in contemporary consumer societies.
Dr Graham Tomlin, Principal, St Paul's Theological Centre,
Holy Trinity Brompton, London

An excellent book: well researched, tellingly illustrated and power-fully but lovingly argued.
Revd Julian Hardyman, Pastor, Eden Baptist Church, Cambridge

The London Lectures in Contemporary Christianity

This is an annual series of lectures founded in 1974 to promote Christian thought about contemporary issues. Their aim is to expound an aspect of historical biblical Christianity and to relate it to a contemporary issue in the church in the world. They seek to be scholarly in content yet popular enough in appeal and style to attract the educated public; and to present each topic in such a way as to be of interest to the widest possible audience as well as to the Christian public.

Previous Lectures:

1997 'Matters of Life and Death: Contemporary medical dilemmas in the light of the Christian faith', *Professor John Wyatt* (published by IVP in 1998 as *Matters of Life and Death: Today's healthcare dilemmas in the light of Christian faith*)

1998 'Endless Conflict or Empty Tolerance: The Christian response to a multi-faith world', *Dr Vinoth Ramachandra* (published by IVP in 1999 as *Faiths in Conflict: Christian integrity in a multicultural world*)

(1999 'Justice That Restores', *Charles Colson* [lectures not delivered, but published by IVP in 2000 as *Justice that Restores*])

2000 'The Incomparable Christ: Celebrating his millennial birth', *John Stott* (published by IVP in 2001 as *The Incomparable Christ*)

2001 'Moral Leadership', *Bishop James Jones* (published by IVP in 2002 as *The Moral Leader: For the church and the world*)

2002 'Moving Genes: Evolving promise or un-natural selection?', *John Bryant* (published by IVP in 2004 as *Life in our Hands: A Christian perspective on genetics and cloning*)

2003 'Can Christianity and Islam Co-exist in the 21st Century?', *Professor Peter G. Riddell* (published by IVP in 2004 as *Christians and Muslims: Pressures and potential in a post-9/11 world*)

2004 'Spirituality, Christianity and the Future of the World', *Dr John Drane* (published by Darton, Longman and Todd as *Do Christians Know How to be Spiritual?*)

2006 'Redeeming Family', *Revd Andrew and Revd Lis Goddard* (publication imminent)

The London Lectures Trust

The London Lectures in Contemporary Christianity are organized by the London Lectures Trust, which was established as a charity in 1994. The committee represents several different evangelical organizations.

Graham Cray

Disciples & Citizens

A vision for
DISTINCTIVE
living

The London Lectures in
Contemporary
Christianity

Inter-Varsity Press
Norton Street, Nottingham NG7 3HR, England
Email: ivp@ivpbooks.com
Website: www.ivpbooks.com

First published 2007

British Library Cataloguing in Publication Data
A catalogue record for this book is available from the British Library.

ISBN: 978-1-84474-157-1

Set in Dante 10.5/13pt
Typeset in Great Britain by CRB Associates, Reepham, Norfolk
Printed and bound in Great Britain by Ashford Colour Press Ltd,
Gosport, Hampshire

Inter-Varsity Press publishes Christian books that are true to the Bible and
that communicate the gospel, develop discipleship and strengthen the
church for its mission in the world.

Inter-Varsity Press is closely linked with the Universities and Colleges
Christian Fellowship, a student movement connecting Christian Unions
in universities and colleges throughout Great Britain, and a member
movement of the International Fellowship of Evangelical Students.
Website: www.uccf.org.uk

For Jackie, Catherine and Sarah,
with grateful thanks for all they have
shown me about being Christian citizens

Contents

Introduction

How should we live as 'dual citizens', citizens both of the kingdom of God and of our nation, in a rapidly changing world? In the light of the kingdom of God, what would be an appropriate Christian involvement in society and its public life?

Many Christians find integrated, whole-life discipleship very difficult. It is easier to live not so much a double life, but a dualistic one, where faith is a personal matter which has very little impact on work, civic participation and other more public areas of life. This is not necessarily hypocritical. Some Christians feel powerless to make any significant difference in the world and decide to keep their heads down, rather than get themselves into difficulty for little or no purpose. Others simply don't know what to do.

Some have an over-negative view of society, combined with an inadequate grasp of the gospel. In fact, this approach is based on a 'double negative': the world 'doesn't really matter' and 'it's bad anyway', and so should be avoided as much as possible. From this point of view, this world's only importance is to provide the context for evangelism, as the gospel is solely about heaven when we die. On the other hand, when society is examined, it is seen as a dangerous place, going from bad to worse: something for 'spiritual' Christians to avoid.

Mercifully, such attitudes are much less prevalent than they once were, thanks in part to initiatives like the London Lectures in Contemporary Christianity. But they have by no means disappeared from the churches. Both forms of dualism are based on an inadequate grasp of Scripture.

As we shall see, there are profound gospel reasons for taking seriously both our national life and our call to be Christian citizens. There are also good reasons for identifying the positive as well as the negative aspects of society. This book will identify ways in which our social health is under threat, but it will do so assuming that a nation's social health is a proper matter of Christian action and concern, because it matters to God.

Graham Cray, Bishop of Maidstone
March 2007

Section One

Citizenship Today

1 Civic responsibility

It takes only a moment's thought to see that the public life of our nation is a proper matter for Christian concern, and a proper setting for Christian discipleship. As residents we want our neighbourhoods to be secure and safe. As parents we want our children to have a good and appropriate education. As patients we want good health-care. As workers we want a fair wage. When we retire we want to be financially secure. When we are old we want to be cared for and treated with dignity. As citizens we want a say in who makes the decisions which have an impact on our lives. As wage earners we are concerned about the level of taxation and how our taxes are spent. All these issues are part of the public life of our nation and proper matters of Christian concern.

As Christians, however, we have an additional dimension. Christian discipleship is not about self-interest. It is about looking to the interests of others. Jesus calls us to love our neighbours as ourselves, and to treat others as we hope to be treated. So it becomes a matter of simple Christian obedience that we should want for others the things we want for ourselves and our own families. If we are willing to act to secure or safeguard these things for ourselves, we should also, at the very least, be willing to act to secure them for others, particularly those weaker than ourselves. If we take the example and teaching of Jesus at all seriously, we may well need to campaign for justice for others, at a cost to ourselves. This, we shall see, takes us to the heart of citizenship: a willingness, for justice's sake, to support actions and policies which are for the greater good, even though personally we might lose out.

The greatest good that any person can encounter is to become a follower of Jesus Christ, finding salvation in him. If we love our neighbours, we will bear witness to them. But witness to Christ involves being an example, embodying what he did and taught into our daily lives. He fed the hungry and healed the sick. He included excluded people. He had a special concern for the poor and, contrary to his culture, treated women and children with the same dignity as men. He challenged unjust leaders and religious hypocrites. This is the Jesus our neighbours need to know and follow.

Because Jesus gave such clear teaching about money, power, faithful relationships, reconciliation, the dignity of children, the love of our neighbour and so on, the state of our society is a proper matter of Christian concern. The growing gap between rich and poor, both nationally and globally, should concern us. Global warming should concern those who believe that God created them to be stewards of the earth. War and terrorism should concern followers of the Prince of Peace. An increasing rate of marriage breakdown should concern those who are called the bride of Christ. Social trends matter in the light of the gospel.

Of course, it is not only Christians who face challenges about civic responsibility. At the time of writing, British public life is, in many ways, positive and full of potential. There are many places around the world where Christian and non-Christian citizens alike would love to have our levels of equality, democratic institutions, social stability, personal freedom and civic institutions.

The research carried out for the Economic and Social Research Council's 'Democracy and Participation' programme[1] concluded that, on the whole, Britons identify with their country and still maintain significant levels of mutual trust. Levels of trust in key unelected institutions, such as the police and the courts, are comparatively high, if uneven, across the whole population. On the other hand, there is much less trust in elected officials, whether local or national. We seem to trust the people we pay, through our taxes, much more than the people we elect to lead us.

Within limits, most citizens show tolerance towards people with whom and organizations with which they would not personally identify. We want a free country and recognize that this must allow people the freedom to do things we would not do ourselves, provided there are proper moral boundaries. (Just what these boundaries are is a matter of debate in a free country.) Although most people believe that government is not very responsive to them as individuals, they do believe that it is responsive to majority opinion. To that degree, civic participation is healthy, but, says the research, 'there is also evidence of a darker side to citizenship'.[2]

The detailed evidence for this 'darker side' will make up the substance for Section Two of this book, but at this point it is worth noticing that citizenship education has only been a required part of the National Curriculum in maintained secondary schools since September 2002. We used to absorb the privileges and duties of citizenship from our culture as a whole, with only a limited amount needing to be part of the school curriculum, but now it is an educational requirement.

According to the Department for Education and Skills,

Three inter-related components that should run through all education for Citizenship [are]:

- Social and moral responsibility:
Pupils learning – from the very beginning – self-confidence and socially and morally responsible behaviour, towards those in authority and towards each other,
- Community involvement:
Pupils learning about becoming helpfully involved in the life and concerns of their neighbourhood and communities,
- Political literacy:
Pupils learning about the institutions, problems and practices of our democracy and how to make themselves effective in the life of the nation, locally, regionally and nationally through skills and values as well as knowledge.[3]

Schools have always been one of the key institutions for teaching young people how to live responsibly in society, alongside the family, the local community and a whole range of voluntary organizations. But the sharpening up of this role and the identification of citizenship as an explicit curriculum subject clearly show that the older processes for citizenship education, where it was more caught than taught, are in difficulties. This has much more to do with the impact of substantial and complex social change than it does with any alleged failure to maintain standards. The context in which we live as citizens has changed substantially.

Social change: citizenship in question

A whole new set of questions cluster around the theme of citizenship today.

Of what are we citizens? Are we citizens of our nations, in this case England, Northern Ireland, Scotland and Wales, or of our state, the United Kingdom? (The *Citizenship in Britain* research found that people identified much more with their nation than with their state.) In what sense are we citizens of Europe or the European Economic Community? In what sense are we citizens of a globalized world? For Christians there are two additional questions. How does all this relate to my loyalty to the worldwide church? How does my loyalty to Christ's global church relate to my responsibilities as a citizen?

How do my rights as a citizen match my responsibilities? Our culture is increasingly strong on rights and weak on matching responsibilities. This is not just a Christian perception. I recently heard a military commander express his concern that the armed forces now drew their recruits from a culture which emphasized individual rights over collective responsibility. Central European human rights legislation is making a substantial impact upon life in the UK, while at the same time there is a trend to devolve responsibility more locally.

What is the value base for citizenship? We are an increasingly diverse and, in some areas, multicultural population. Globally both the affluent and the poor are increasingly mobile. The affluent are mobile because of the multinational basis of commerce and because they have the resources to be mobile. The poor, and minority groups, are forced to be mobile because of their poverty, becoming economic migrants, or out of fear for their own safety, if they do not find sanctuary elsewhere, as asylum seekers. Immigrants, refugees and asylum seekers raise questions of national identity and the expectations of responsible citizenship.

In democratic societies citizens have traditionally expected their governments to keep them safe. Security has been one of the potential added values of national identity. Since the destruction of New York's Twin Towers on 9/11, all Western societies have been in anxious debate about the price of security in terms of restrictions on personal liberties. In the UK this was reinforced by the London bombings of July 2005. 'Free' and 'citizen' no longer sit so comfortably together.

Understandings of the rights and responsibilities of citizenship also come under pressure through the growing inequality which is a characteristic of consumer societies. The poor or marginalized always want the state to interfere more, whereas the comfortable want it to interfere less! The whole issue also needs to be put into proportion by setting it in its proper context of the global disparity between rich and poor nations.

Citizenship is becoming increasingly passive. Most citizens benefit from their membership of society, but there is a substantial decline in the proportion of citizens who vote, or who think voting makes any difference. Perhaps most serious of all is the decline in concern for or confidence in the concept of the 'common good'. There has been a 'hollowing out' of the public sphere,[4] an undermining of confidence in the public interest, as distinct from private or commercial interests, which is a great matter of concern. The public square has become far too much a competitive marketplace between private interests, single-issue groups and commercial interests, rather than a place where all of these take second place to the greater good. It is precisely at this point that Christians, and other people of faith, have a substantial contribution to make.

These are all complex issues, each meriting a book in their own right, and I shall not attempt to address them directly. I shall, however, attempt to set out a Christian perspective on citizenship as public discipleship, from which these issues can be addressed.

Citizenship defined

Before going any further I need to give some definition to citizenship. *Citizenship in Britain* uses this definition: 'Citizenship is a set of norms, values and practices, designed to solve collective action problems which involve the recognition by individuals that they have rights and obligations to each other if they wish to solve such problems.'[5] This is hardly a definition to set the heart racing! But it identifies key elements, including a sense of mutual responsibility and a willingness to act for the common good.

The challenge of citizenship, however, is not about a definition. It is about our capacity to be the sort of people citizenship requires. The key to citizenship is getting people to act for the common good when they might not benefit themselves, to recognize obligations as well as rights. It is about generating shared values and also developing sufficient character to live by them. 'There must be a degree of consensus over the values that underpin citizenship, if modern societies are not to fragment further, and thereby become increasingly hard to govern effectively.'[6] The difficulty is that there are powerful social trends moving us away from that necessary level of consensus.

> Changes in British society in the late twentieth and early twenty-first centuries are making the conditions for cooperative action relatively harder to achieve over time. This is because Britain is now a rapidly changing, multicultural society, with a lot of geographical mobility and diverse values. The long term changes in attitudes and behaviour are moving us in the direction of declining collective participation and weakening social norms.[7]

These changes provide the current context of discussion about citizenship.

Having offered a definition, *Citizenship in Britain* goes on to say, 'The state is essentially the transmission mechanism for these values and practices *rather than the source of them*, although state action can contribute both to their promotion and to their destruction.'[8] So where do our values come from? Where and how are they generated? It is the issue of values, and of character, which will become a central concern of this book. Our nation needs a vision of the public good, combined with a proportionate willingness for self-sacrifice.

As citizens, Christians need to respond to these challenges. Although we are a pluralist society, we will serve our nation and world best by being ourselves, by offering our nation a genuinely biblical vision.

Notes

1 Published as Charles Pattie, Patrick Seyd and Paul Whiteley, *Citizenship in Britain*, Cambridge: Cambridge University Press, 2004.

2 Ibid., p. 267.

3 See www.dfes.gov.uk/citizenship.

4 David Marquand, *The Decline of the Public – The Hollowing Out of Citizenship*, Cambridge: Polity Press, 2004.

5 Pattie et al., *Citizenship*, p. 22.

6 Keith Faulks, *Citizenship*, London: Routledge, 2000, p. 164.

7 Pattie et al., *Citizenship*, p. 280.

8 Ibid., p. 22, italics mine.

Citizenship in the light of the
2 New Testament

Some presuppositions

Christians are dual citizens of the kingdom of God and of their respective nations. The key question is, how are these dual loyalties to be held together in a coherent and integrated way of life? The first Christian creed was 'Jesus is Lord' and the lordship of Christ over the whole created order is the inevitable and proper starting point for all Christian engagement with society. 'Jesus came and said to them, "All authority in heaven and on earth has been given to me"' (Matt. 28:18). Paul makes similar claims about the universal rule of Christ. 'For in him all things in heaven and on earth were created, things visible and invisible, whether thrones or dominions or rulers or powers – all things have been created through him and for him. He himself is before all things, and in him all things hold together' (Col. 1:16–17). So the question of dual citizenship cannot be resolved by dividing life into a sphere where Christ rules and another where we operate according to different principles. Discipleship is to be lived out in every dimension of life. The Christian term for citizenship is, in effect, public discipleship.

This can bring Christians into conflict with their societies, when the values of society and the values of Christ's kingdom conflict. But it does not set Christians over against their societies, as public discipleship seeks the common good, in the light of the kingdom of God. This was beautifully expressed in the best-known section of the second-century Epistle to Diognetus.

> For the Christians are distinguished from other men neither by country, nor language, nor the customs which they observe. For they neither inhabit cities of their own, nor employ a peculiar form of speech, nor lead a life which is marked out by any singularity ... But, inhabiting Greek as well as barbarian cities, according as the lot of each of them has determined, and following the customs of the natives in respect to clothing, food, and the rest of their ordinary conduct, they display to us their wonderful and confessedly striking method of life. They dwell in their own countries, but simply as sojourners. As citizens, they share in all things with others, and yet endure all things as if foreigners. Every foreign land is to them as their native country, and every land of their birth as a land of strangers. They marry, as do all [others]; they beget children; but they do not destroy their offspring. They have a common table, but not a common bed. They are in the flesh, but they do not live after the flesh. They pass their days on earth, but they are citizens of heaven. They obey the prescribed laws, and at the same time surpass the laws by their lives ... To sum up all in one word – what the soul is in the body, that are Christians in the world.

Evangelical approaches to citizenship

Evangelical Christians have always agreed that the lordship of Christ is the foundation stone of any Christian understanding of the state and of our obligation to it. They have not always agreed as to what that means in practice. Underlying these differences have been different understandings of the kingdom of God.

1. The quietist approach – the kingdom is primarily future
Some trends within evangelicalism, particularly from an earlier generation, have tended to be negative towards society, with a

world-escaping emphasis. Priority was given to those texts which identify the 'world' with its negative meaning of society organized apart from God. 'Do you not know that friendship with the world is enmity with God? Therefore whoever wishes to be a friend of the world becomes an enemy of God' (Jas 4:4). In 1 John we read, 'Do not love the world or the things in the world. The love of the Father is not in those who love the world; for all that is in the world – the desire of the flesh, the desire of the eyes, the pride in riches, comes not from the Father but from the world. And the world and its desire are passing away, but those who do the will of God live forever' (1 John 2:15–17). Here 'the world' and human society are treated as identical. Society is thus seen as primarily a corrupting influence, from which Christians should withdraw for their own spiritual purity. 'World' in this negative sense means the way in which the fallen human race lives apart from God. It describes a wrong way of living on the earth, which Christians should not share. But the New Testament just as often uses the term 'world' to mean either the earth, the created order, or the human community. In both of these cases the emphasis is on God's love for, and commitment to, his world, despite its fallen state.[1] As we shall see, Christian citizenship calls for an active but distinctive engagement with society, not a withdrawal for one's own spiritual protection.

Although this tendency is not as strong as it used to be, it has a long history and remains a temptation for some. Sir Fred Catherwood's classic volume *The Christian Citizen* argued that 'the Christian should be actively concerned with and involved in the world outside the church'[2] and against a 'doctrine of rigid separation from the world', which, as he said, outsiders found hard to distinguish 'from an attitude of indifference to the world and its problems'.[3]

Once this negative attitude to society is accepted, Christian citizenship is reduced to the question of obedience to the state. Romans 13 became the proof text for a combination of non-involvement, keeping one's head down and always obeying the authorities, unless they forbade you to preach the gospel, as in Acts 4.[4]

A careful reading of Romans 13:1–7 does not support this interpretation. While supporting the vocation of the state, as instituted by God, to maintain what is good and to punish wrongdoing for the common good ('for your good', v. 4), Paul reduces its scope in a way that the Roman administration would have considered unacceptable. When Paul was writing, the cult of the emperor was growing. From Paul's perspective, Caesar may consider himself divine, but he is only a servant, put in place by God for a limited purpose. He and his administration are accountable to God's final judgment just like anyone else. He is to be paid his due, whether by paying taxes or being law abiding, but no more (v. 7).

Paul's experience of the state was very different from our understanding of nation states. In a democratic society, Christians will have a more proactive role in challenging the state when it steps beyond its God-given vocation than was possible for the first-century church. However, Paul is quite clear about the subversive nature of Christian discipleship. In verse 8 he instructs the Roman Christians to 'owe no one anything, except to love one another'. As we shall see, this is not primarily about not getting into debt, but about a refusal to abide by the client-and-patron system which was endemic to Roman culture and was the way in which the empire operated. Romans 13 is a subversive text from the empire's point of view.

Paul is not naïve. He sees government as a good gift of God, so its role is to be honoured. But he does not assume that a pagan state is benign. The break between chapters 12 and 13 is unfortunate. Paul's directions about attitude to the Roman government begin with the words, 'Do not be overcome by evil, but overcome evil with good' (Rom. 12:21).

We find similar teaching in 1 Peter.

> Beloved, I urge you as aliens and exiles to abstain from the desires of the flesh that wage war against the soul. Conduct yourselves honourably among the Gentiles, so that, though they malign you as evildoers, they may see your honourable deeds and glorify God when he comes to judge.
>
> For the Lord's sake accept the authority of every human institution, whether of the emperor as supreme, or of governors, as sent by him to punish those who do wrong and to praise those who do right. For it is God's will that by doing right you should silence the ignorance of the foolish. As servants of God, live as free people, yet do not use your freedom as a pretext for evil. Honour everyone. Love the family of believers. Fear God. Honour the emperor.
>
> (1 Pet. 2:11–17)

Here Christians are seen as 'resident aliens'. In a context of per-secution they accept proper human authority 'for the Lord's sake'. They are servants of God who also give the emperor the level of honour he is due. Despite false accusations and potential injustice, their attitude to society is to bless it. As far as they are able, they do more than what the law identifies as 'right'. They are to honour their fellow citizens and do 'honourable deeds'.

Where Christian citizenship is reduced merely to respect for the authorities, there is often an inadequate understanding of the kingdom of God close to hand. Jesus' statement before Pilate that 'my kingdom is not from this world' (John 18:36) is misread as saying 'my kingdom is not about this world', rather than 'my kingdom does not originate from this world'. The kingdom is seen as the inner rule of Christ in this life, as an anticipation of his eternal rule in heaven. But God's kingdom is his reign over *all* things which cannot be limited to his inner reign in the hearts of those who believe. 'Neither in Judaism nor elsewhere in the New Testament do we find that the reign of God is something indwelling in men, to be found, say, in the heart; such a spiritualistic understanding is ruled out both for Jesus and for the early Christian tradition.'[5] When Jesus taught his disciples to pray 'your kingdom come', he gave them a supplementary clause: 'your will be done on earth as in heaven'.

2. The transformational approach – the kingdom has a transformative impact on the present

Other evangelicals have shown a better grasp of the breadth of Jesus' teaching on the kingdom, with its instruction on lifestyle and its concern for the poor and excluded. They have also seen scriptural material about slavery, the role of women and other issues as a springboard for long-term social change.

Even here, however, there has been a tendency to concentrate on specific social issues without always giving adequate attention to the underlying shape of the Christian hope as a basis for our engage-ment with society. Central to this shape is the connection between our actions now and the future God has promised. It is this relationship which provides the basis for all Christian engagement with society.

The future in the present

The unprecedented aspect of Jesus' understanding of the kingdom was that the future rule of God was in some sense present now. This effected a 'decisive shift in eschatology from the future above, to the future in the present'.[6] Instead of the new age replacing the old in one final act of judgment, as Jesus' contemporaries expected, it had invaded it without totally displacing it. God's promised future had arrived in Christ, but was not yet complete. 'Christ has cleft the future in two, and part of it is already present.'[7] In common with the Jews of his day, Jesus still saw human history as divided between two ages, but the critical dividing point (*kairos*) was not the final judgment, but his own proclamation and ministry. 'The time is fulfilled, and the kingdom of God has come near' (Mark 1:15).

From the time of Jesus' public ministry, especially his atoning death and resurrection, until the judgment, the ages are in overlap. As a consequence, the kingdom of God should be understood as 'the presence of the future'.[8] It still awaits its consummation and thus has to be understood as both 'already' and 'not yet'.

Christians are to live on the earth in the light of God's future and in the power of God's future (the Holy Spirit). 'To be a Christian, a person of faith, is precisely to live as a person for whom God's future shapes the present.'[9] If the kingdom of God is both already and not yet, then there is clearly an element of continuity between the life and witness of Christians now and the kingdom in its ultimate fullness. Christians live in the present, in the light of the future which Christ secured in the past. The implications of this theological framework will be explored in greater detail in the final section of this book. It is enough, for the moment, to note that the implications are for the whole of life. If citizenship is public discipleship, that discipleship acknowledges no compartmentalizing into public versus private, or sacred versus secular, as though the future which Christ has secured only had an impact on certain compartments and not on others.

Christian social, ethical and political commitments are teleological. They are imperfect anticipations of a promised future. We are to live our public as well as our private lives in the light of that future.

Notes

1 See David Wells, *God in the Wasteland*, Leicester: IVP, 1994, p. 37.

2 Sir Frederick Catherwood, *The Christian Citizen*, London: Hodder & Stoughton, 1969, p. 11.

3 Ibid., p. 17.

4 Acts 4:18: 'So they called them and ordered them not to speak or teach at all in the name of Jesus. But Peter and John answered them, "Whether it is right in God's sight to listen to you rather than to God, you must judge; for we cannot keep from speaking about what we have seen and heard." '

5 Jeremias, *New Testament Theology – The Proclamation of Jesus*, London: SCM, 1971, p. 101.

6 G. R. Beasley-Murray, *Jesus and the Kingdom of God*, Exeter: Paternoster, 1986, p. 338.

7 David Bosch, 'Evangelism and Social Transformation', in Tom Sine (ed.), *The Church in Response to Human Need*, Monrovia: Marc, 1983, p. 277f.

8 George Eldon Ladd, *The Presence of the Future*, London: SPCK, 1974.

9 Richard Bauckham and Trevor Hart, *Hope Against Hope*, London: Darton, Longman & Todd, 1999, p. 83.

3 A case study from Corinth[1]

The framework for hope and principled involvement in society mentioned above can be illustrated very clearly from Paul's first letter to the Corinthians, with occasional supporting reference to his other letters.

Why Corinth?

At first glance, 1 Corinthians seems a strange choice as a source relevant to contemporary dilemmas. The culture of ancient Corinth was indeed very different from contemporary Western societies, but a closer look also reveals striking similarities.

Corinth was 'one of the truly great cities of the Roman world'. It was a Roman colony created by order of Julius Caesar. By Paul's time it was well on the way to being the largest and most prosperous city in Greece, with a population of 70–80,000 people. Located on a narrow isthmus, it formed the meeting point of the eastern and western halves of the Roman Empire, with a port on each coast. The city was famous for its Isthmian Games, second in fame only to the

Olympics, which were held every two years, including AD 51 when Paul was there. The population was thus cosmopolitan and pluralist and included a large Jewish community, which had been swollen when Claudius expelled the Jews from Rome. There was a diverse range of religions and cults, although the imperial cult was growing in influence.

Corinth attracted travellers, traders and tourists. It was prosperous through imports from East and West, and had a thriving 'economy of market exchange of goods and services'. The city offered ample opportunities for migrants, and was 'a magnet for the socially ambitious'. 'Entrepreneurial pragmatism' was seen as the key to success. At the same time, the city could not grow enough crops on the isthmus to support its whole population. The poor lived with the danger of famine whenever the market price of corn got too high.

The key to financial and social success was the system of patronage. The culture of the aspiring or the well-to-do was dominated by a desire to advance up the social ladder. Many people sought a patron who could take them further up that ladder, in return for services rendered. Status was everything, so self-promotion was endemic. Corinth was 'a society preoccupied with concern for public status, honour and self-promotion'. 'Public recognition was often more important than facts.' 'A person's sense of worth was based on recognition by others of one's accomplishments.' The ambitious looked 'not for truth but for applause and success'. There was an 'obsession with peer group prestige' and 'near contempt for those without standing in some chosen value system'.

As a consequence, Corinth was 'a city where public boasting and self-promotion had become an art form'.[2] A first-century cult of celebrity took shape from 'a drive for adulation'. This found particular expression in two first-century forms of communication. Public inscriptions promoting the significance of different well-to-do citizens have been discovered at the site of ancient Corinth in 'staggering numbers'. Corinth also provided a veritable honeypot for professional public speakers. Highly trained in various forms of rhetoric, these 'sophists' ('wise men') were employed to promote the cause, reputation and ambitions of whoever paid them. They were the spin doctors of ancient Corinth, employed to manipulate and shape popular perceptions. As we shall see, this is why Paul, whose letters demonstrate a knowledge of rhetoric, was so careful to avoid the techniques of professional public speakers in his ministry in the city.

Contemporary parallels

Corinth was a materially ambitious, multicultural city. It was governed by personal ambition and self-promotion, sustained by a culture of spin. 'Corinthian culture has much in common with the social constructivism, competitive pragmatism and radical pluralism which characterizes so-called postmodernity as a popular mood.'[3] Another contemporary parallel was the huge disparity between rich and poor.

The church in Corinth was mixed and socially diverse. The urban poor, including slaves, probably made up the majority of the community numerically,[4] but a significant minority were wealthy and some played a full part in their civic society's status and patronage games. It was this group who caused a number of the problems which Paul addresses in this letter.

Others made their resources available to Christ's work, and hosted the church. It is interesting that the three whom Paul names appear to be from different racial groups. Gaius is a Roman name, Stephanas a Greek name, and Crispus is Jewish. So here is a church and a culture very different from our own, yet facing strikingly similar challenges.

What does Paul's seemingly disparate advice about a range of issues, many of which we find culturally strange, have to teach us?

The significance of the resurrection

The first letter to the Corinthians culminates in an extensive chapter on the nature and significance of the resurrection of Christ. Chapter 15 towers over the whole letter. It provides not merely the final issue to be addressed, but the key underlying conviction which gives coherence to all the diverse teaching on discipleship throughout the letter.

In this chapter the resurrection provides a vision of this life in the light of the next. The future includes not only a personal resurrection, but an era in which Christ rules over the whole creation, without any enemy resisting him. It is this hope which makes the hard work of serving God worthwhile.

> If for this life only we have hoped in Christ, we are of all people most to be pitied.
>
> But in fact Christ has been raised from the dead, the first fruits of those who have died. For since death came through a human being, the resurrection of the dead has also come through a human being; for as all die in Adam, so all will be made alive in Christ. But each in his own order: Christ the first fruits, then at his coming those who belong to Christ. Then comes the end, when he hands over the kingdom to God the Father, after he has destroyed every ruler and every authority and power. For he must reign until he has put all his enemies under his feet. The last enemy to be destroyed is death. For 'God has put all things in subjection under his feet.' But when it says, 'All things are put in subjection,' it is plain that this does not include the one who put all things in subjection under him ... Therefore, my beloved, be steadfast, immovable, always excelling in the work of the Lord, because you know that in the Lord your labour is not in vain.
> (1 Cor. 15:19–27, 58)

In the light of this future hope, the strategy for public discipleship which Paul commends can be identified under two headings: 'involved distinctiveness' and 'subversive engagement'. These two combine to create a nuanced approach to Christian involvement in society, for public discipleship. They are not so much separate categories as complementary emphases.

Involved distinctiveness

Involved distinctiveness can be summed up as a call to be a counter-cultural community which also seeks common ground with its society whenever possible. This community is to be involved in, rather than withdrawn from, society.

Countercultural community

The Corinthian church had to be countercultural to survive. There is little reference in the letter to direct physical persecution or theological doubts which might result in a believer turning away from the new faith (although there was plenty of wrong-headed theology which led directly to inappropriate decisions about lifestyle and discipleship). Rather, it was social pressure that caused the problems. 'It was not a change of heart that might win a Christian convert back to paganism, but the overwhelming pressure to conform imposed by the institutions of his city and the activities of his neighbour.'[5] Few individual Christians could withstand that pressure. What was needed was a distinctively Christian community.

Moral behaviour

The primary distinctiveness was to be a moral one. Appropriate distinctiveness was identified in the light of the kingdom of God, which had broken through in Christ and which would be brought to completion when he appeared. So Paul wrote, 'Do you not know that wrongdoers will not inherit the kingdom of God? Do not be deceived! Fornicators, idolaters, adulterers, male prostitutes, sodomites, thieves, the greedy, drunkards, revilers, robbers – none of these will inherit the kingdom of God' (1 Cor. 6:9–10). God's future world had clear moral qualities and conversion implied a moral transformation. Paul recognizes the way in which this transforming power of the gospel had already been at work in Corinth. 'And this is what some of you used to be. But you were washed, you were sanctified, you were justified in the name of the Lord Jesus Christ and in the Spirit of our God' (6:11).

This transformation, and this particular list of previous sinful behaviour, clearly applied to the full social range within the Corinthian church. Other advice had particular reference to the more influential minority.

Paul wrote 1 Corinthians in response to a letter from the church at Corinth. In chapter 6, Paul quotes for the first time a key expression used in that letter as a justification for some of the behaviour he wished to challenge: 'All things are lawful for me' (6:12a[6]) – in effect, 'I am free to do anything.' Paul replies, 'But not all things are beneficial. "All things are lawful for me," but I will not be dominated by anything' (6:12b). He then applies this principle to food and to sexual sin.

> 'Food is meant for the stomach and the stomach for food,' and God will destroy both one and the other. The body is meant not for fornication but for the Lord, and the Lord for the body. And God raised the Lord and will also raise us by his power. Do you not know that your bodies are members of Christ? Should I therefore take the members of Christ and make them members of a prostitute? Never! Do you not know that whoever is united to a prostitute becomes one body with her? For it is said, 'The two shall be one flesh.' But anyone united to the Lord becomes one spirit with him. Shun fornication! Every sin that a person commits is outside the body; but the fornicator sins against the body itself. Or do you not know that your body is a temple of the Holy Spirit within you, which you have from God, and that you are not your own? For you were bought with a price; therefore glorify God in your body.
>
> (1 Cor. 6:13–20)

There is clear general teaching here about gluttony and fornication, but Paul also has a particular social pressure in mind.[7] Ancient Corinth had been notorious for its sexual immorality and Roman Corinth offered a range of sexual experience typical of such seaports and large cities. Yet it is not even the general availability of brothels which Paul has in mind, but social norms about private banquets. 'The elite who gave private banquets, to which they invited clients (those socially dependent upon them) as well as other guests, provided not only for their physical hunger but also for their sexual appetites.'[8] This was achieved through the provision of a travelling brothel. Well-to-do members of the Corinthian congregation would be invited to such events, as would those who were clients to pagan patrons. Young men were particularly vulnerable. They received their Roman *toga virilis*, their coming of age, at eighteen, and were then eligible for such invitations, where they would learn 'to be men'. They were, in effect, being introduced into a life of promiscuity by both choice and convention, with social pressure, connected to a civic right, tempting them to depart from Christian chastity.

This surrender to social pressure was justified by an inadequate theology. Distinctive Christian behaviour was being undermined by a failure to engage in distinctive Christian thinking. Some members of the church were giving uncritical acceptance to the Greek doctrine of the immortality of the soul. They assumed that only the spiritual, as opposed to the physical, could survive to the next life, and as a result the body could be indulged, whether through gluttony or sexual intercourse, as it would only exist in this life and what was done in it had no eternal significance. Christian liberty is thus treated as a licence for licence! Paul points out that their bodies are members of Christ and temples of the Holy Spirit. This is the same Holy (morally pure) Spirit by whom Jesus' body was raised and by whom our bodies will also be raised and transformed on the last day.

Rights

Much like today, Corinth was a rights culture. The well-to-do knew their rights and insisted on them. Within the church this led to confusion between civic rights and Christian freedom. Many civic occasions took place in pagan temples. Paul was not particularly concerned about Christians eating meat which had been used in sacrifice (see 10:25), probably the only meat generally available in the markets, but he was highly concerned about Christians participating in idolatrous worship, or even appearing to do so. He was also concerned about the use of personal rights irrespective of the impact on others.

> But take care that this liberty of yours does not somehow become a stumbling block to the weak. For if others see you, who possess knowledge, eating in the temple of an idol, might they not, since their conscience is weak, be encouraged to the point of eating food sacrificed to idols?
> (1 Cor. 8:9–10)

By their 'liberty' he meant their right to attend. Paul might well have said, 'You don't have a right to sin, or to cause other Christians to go against their consciences.' Paul's main argument about people's 'rights', whether in Christ or as citizens, is that they are not for one's own benefit, but always to be used for the benefit of others. If a choice between personal rights and the benefit of others has to be made, it is personal rights that are to be sacrificed. The argument concerning the personal civic right of the Corinthians that 'all things are lawful' is countered by Paul's argument concerning the welfare of others: 'Not all things are beneficial.' 'The pursuit of one's rights on the ground that it is lawful, cannot be undertaken at the same time as the pursuit of the welfare of all.'[9]

The basis for ethics is not knowledge of our rights, but love tangibly expressed to others. 'Knowledge puffs up, but love builds up' (1 Cor. 8:1). 'It is not a matter of whether one has the freedom or the right to do something, whether it is justifiable, but of whether it is for the common good.'[10]

Christians, then, are to be morally distinctive as much in public as in private, concerned about the welfare of others rather than their own rights and privileges.

Discernment based on the vision of the future secured by Christ

This practical discernment about lifestyle is based on a vision of the future that Christ has secured. Crudely put, the underlying principle is that behaviour which has no place in God's future is not acceptable now. This is spelled out throughout 1 Corinthians. The only things that can survive are those which are both built on the foundation of Christ and able to survive the fire of God's final testing.

> According to the grace of God given to me, like a skilled master builder I laid a foundation, and someone else is building on it. Each builder must choose with care how to build on it. For no one can lay any foundation other than the one that has been laid; that foundation is Jesus Christ. Now if anyone builds on the foundation with gold, silver, precious stones, wood, hay, straw – the work of each builder will become visible, for the Day will disclose it, because it will be revealed with fire, and the fire will test what sort of work each has done. If what has been built on the foundation survives, the builder will receive a reward. If the work is burned up, the builder will suffer loss; the builder will be saved, but only as through fire.
> (1 Cor. 3:10–15)

When Paul contrasts the 'flesh' and the 'spirit', he is not so much speaking of two dimensions within us as making the contrast between this age, which is passing away, and the future which Christ has inaugurated.

> And so, brothers and sisters, I could not speak to you as spiritual people, but rather as people of the flesh, as infants in Christ . . . for you are still of the flesh. For as long as there is jealousy and quarrelling among you, are you not of the flesh, and behaving according to human inclinations? For when one says, 'I belong to Paul,' and another, 'I belong to Apollos,' are you not merely human? . . . Do you not know that you are God's temple and that God's Spirit dwells in you?
> (1 Cor. 3:1, 3–4, 16)

In Paul the Holy Spirit is 'the *certain evidence* that the future had dawned, and the *absolute guarantee* of its final consummation'.[11] It is a present-future contrast. We live by human effort, apart from Christ, or by the power of the Spirit.

However impressive its achievements, culture created apart from Christ cannot survive. Christ's coming requires us to make a radical re-evaluation of our society.

> I mean, brothers and sisters, the appointed time [*kairos*] has grown short; from now on, let even those who have wives be as though they had none, and those who mourn as though they were not mourning, and those who rejoice as though they were not rejoicing, and those who buy as though they had no possessions, and those who deal with the world as though they had no dealings with it. For the present form of this world is passing away.
> (1 Cor. 7:29–31)

Paul is not being literal here. He is not saying that the second coming is so near that there is no point doing anything. In the same chapter, he says that husbands and wives should not withdraw from sexual relationships, nor should they divorce. As we shall see, he very specifically challenges any idea of a radical withdrawal from society (see 5:9ff.). He is using hyperbole to make a dramatic point. The coming of Christ has relativized the existing culture. 'Paul's basic strategy at Corinth was to emphasize that eschatological events of the past, present and future had relativized the present world order and that the schema of this world was passing away.'[12] He is providing a theology of the imminence of the end, *not* a chronology of it! 'Paul's concern is not with the amount of time they have left, but with the radical new perspective the "foreshortened future" gives one with regard to the present age.'[13]

The Scriptures are given to the church to help them to live during 'the ends of the ages': 'These things happened to them to serve as an example, and they were written down to instruct us, on whom the ends of the ages have come' (1 Cor. 10:11). That is the era between Christ's ascension and his final appearing.

A visible alternative community

During this interim period, Christians are to live as a visible alternative community. In a city packed with highly visible temples, they were to be the visible temple of the only true God. 'Do you not know that you are God's temple and that God's Spirit dwells in you?' (1 Cor. 3:16) Paul uses the temple metaphor of the whole Christian community (the 'you' in 3:16 is plural) and then applies it to individual Christians (see 6:19). 'As God's temple they are intended to be his alternative to Corinth, to both its religions and vices.'[14]

A clear distinction between the cultural and the ethical

This Christ-shaped distinctiveness, however, is never about being different for difference's sake. A clear distinction is made between ethical behaviour and cultural patterns. In the light of Christ and the gospel proclamation to the Gentiles, even circumcision, once the mark of belonging to God's covenant people, has been reduced to one nation's cultural tradition. 'Circumcision is nothing, and uncircumcision is nothing; but obeying the commandments of God is everything' (1 Cor. 7:19). It is in ethics, not national cultural practices, that distinctiveness is to be seen. In fact, Paul believes that the gospel can take shape within many different cultures. His own example and his practice as an evangelist are to ensure that he does not impose his own culture on those whom he wins for Christ. But he does look for an ethical distinctiveness within each culture, whether Jewish or Gentile.

For though I am free with respect to all, I have made myself a slave to all, so that I might win more of them. To the Jews I became as a Jew, in order to win Jews. To those under the law I became as one under the law (though I myself am not under the law) so that I might win those under the law. To those outside the law I became as one outside the law (though I am not free from God's law but am under Christ's law) so that I might win those outside the law. To the weak I became weak, so that I might win the weak. I have become all things to all people, that I might by all means save some. I do it all for the sake of the gospel, so that I may share in its blessings.

(1 Cor. 9:19–23)

This is more than cultural flexibility. It returns us to the issue of individual rights. 'This passage is often read as a statement of St. Paul's cultural flexibility for the sake of his mission; rightly so, but its deeper point is Paul's willingness to relinquish his own freedom for the sake of the gospel.'[15]

Christian distinctiveness is a vital part of citizenship, of faithful public discipleship, but it is not a distinctiveness set over against others. It is an ethical distinctiveness for the sake of others, to show them a better way, for their own welfare. It is closely linked to a Christian approach to rights, which places them in the service of others, or sets them aside for the sake of others, in the light of the gospel.

Seeking common ground
As such, it is never distinctiveness for its own sake, rather seeking common ground, whenever that can be established with integrity. He challenges the Corinthian church that 'It is actually reported that there is sexual immorality among you, and *of a kind that is not found even among pagans*; for a man is living with his father's wife' (1 Cor. 5:1, my italics). In other words, the church is permitting something that 'everyone knows is wrong'!

Public discipleship involves seeking genuine common ground in ethics with popular society. This can often provide Christian grounding for norms shared with society. Many of Paul's lists of sins (as in 1 Cor. 5:10–11 and 6:9–10) have parallels with Jewish lists and the more ethical end of Greek and Roman ones. Paul knows that people whose minds have been shaped by the law of Moses or certain parts of Greek or Roman philosophy would agree that this sort of behaviour was wrong, even if endemic in society. In Romans 2 he assumes 'a commonly shared sense of what is good':[16]

> When Gentiles, who do not possess the law, do instinctively what the law requires, these, though not having the law, are a law to themselves. They show that what the law requires is written on their hearts, to which their own conscience also bears witness; and their conflicting thoughts will accuse or perhaps excuse them.
> (Rom. 2:14–15)

He frequently refers or appeals to conscience, both within and beyond the Christian community. Romans was written from Corinth and includes the command, 'Do not repay anyone evil for evil, but take thought for what is noble in the sight of all' (12:17).

Christian distinctiveness often lies less in distinctive values than in distinctive living. 'Paul's claim is not so much that Christians live by distinctive ethical standards but rather that they live up to, and beyond, the ethical standards that others share but do not follow.'[17]

Involvement

Whether or not Christian distinctiveness is found in ethical standards or quality of lifestyle, it is an involved distinctiveness, not a detached one. Paul does not call for a social separation from unbelievers. Some in the Corinthian church had misunderstood him on this subject in his previous letter, and he sets the record straight with this clarification.

> I wrote to you in my letter not to associate with sexually immoral persons – not at all meaning the immoral of this world, or the greedy and robbers, or idolaters, since you would then need to go out of the world. But now I am writing to you not to associate with anyone who bears the name of brother or sister who is sexually immoral or greedy, or is an idolater, reviler, drunkard, or robber. Do not even eat with such a one.
> (1 Cor. 5:9–11)

It is Christians who live by a double standard who are to be avoided, not consistent pagans! Christians who live distinctively Christian lives are meant to be rubbing shoulders with people whose current lifestyle would keep them out of the kingdom of heaven.

The tricky issue of whether it was all right to eat meat which had been previously offered to an idol was leading some Christians to refuse all meal invitations from pagans. This was disastrous to mission, because local mission has to be based on the establishing of real relationships. In a culture where hospitality was expressed with food, it was almost impossible to become a friend of someone and refuse to eat with them. Paul's advice is clear.

> If an unbeliever invites you to a meal and you are disposed to go, eat whatever is set before you without raising any question on the ground of conscience. But if someone says to you, 'This has been offered in sacrifice,' then do not eat it, out of consideration for the one who informed you, and for the sake of conscience – I mean the other's conscience, not your own. For why should my liberty be subject to the judgment of someone else's conscience? If I partake with thankfulness, why should I be denounced because of that for which I give thanks?
>
> So, whether you eat or drink, or whatever you do, do everything for the glory of God. Give no offence to Jews or to Greeks or to the church of God.
>
> (1 Cor. 10:27–32)

The meat is not the issue, but rather sensitivity to your host's conscience, so that your friendship has integrity.

As we said at the outset of this section, involved distinctiveness can be summed up as a call to be a countercultural community which also seeks common ground with its society whenever possible – a community involved in, rather than withdrawn from, society. Involved distinctiveness, however, also requires subversive engagement.

Subversive engagement

Subversive engagement involves a proactive community, actively doing good in its society (because the good can last, in the light of the kingdom of God), while subverting many of its society's key social values (because they cannot last, in the light of the kingdom of God).

Doing good

'Do-gooder' is a disparaging term in our society, but it is one ripe for redemption. Public discipleship involves doing good. It involves actively seeking the things that benefit others.

In response to the Corinthian mantra about rights, Paul replies:

> 'All things are lawful,' but not all things are beneficial [for the welfare of others]. 'All things are lawful,' but not all things build up. Do not seek your own advantage, but that of the other . . . Give no offence to Jews or to Greeks or to the church of God, just as I try to please everyone in everything I do, not seeking my own advantage, but that of many, so that they may be saved . . . Be imitators of me, as I am of Christ. (10:23–24, 32–33; 11:1)

It is not only that Christians are to avoid unnecessary offence to unbelievers; they are actively to seek their advantage. Paul sets this out as his own practice and clearly sees no conflict between evangelism and social engagement here. To seek the advantage of another, says Paul, can contribute to their eventual salvation.

The call to show love or do good to all is a consistent theme in Paul's letters. In his earliest letter (1 Thessalonians) he writes, 'And may the Lord make you increase and abound in love for one another and for all' (3:12), and 'See that none of you repays evil for evil, but always seek to do good to one another and to all' (5:15). To the Galatians he says, 'So let us not grow weary in doing what is right, for we will reap at harvest time, if we do not give up. So then, whenever we have an opportunity, let us work for the good of all, and especially for those of the family of faith' (Gal. 6:9–10). Writing from Corinth to the church in Rome, he says, 'Each of us must please our neighbour for the good purpose of building up the neighbour' (Rom. 15:2).

I had always seen Paul's term 'build up' or 'edify' as a term he coined for the purpose of Christian relationships within the church, but he uses it just as often for the way Christians relate to their surrounding society.

Following Jesus, Paul sees such love of neighbour as the fulfilling of God's law.

> The commandments, 'You shall not commit adultery; You shall not murder; You shall not steal; You shall not covet'; and any other commandment, are summed up in this word, 'Love your neighbour as yourself.' Love does no wrong to a neighbour; therefore, love is the fulfilling of the law.
> (Rom. 13:9–10)

> Each of us must please our neighbour for the good purpose of building up the neighbour.
> (Rom. 15:2)

> For the whole law is summed up in a single commandment, 'You shall love your neighbour as yourself.'
> (Gal. 5:14)

We have been so exposed to the idea that we ought to 'love our neighbour as ourselves' that we fail to grasp the revolutionary nature of the suggestion in Corinth. To quote Bruce Winter, 'Roman society was not concerned for neighbours but advantageous networking.'[18]

Empowerment

Paul expected all Christians, rich or poor, weak or strong, to seek the advantage of others: to be 'benefactors' seeking the things that benefit others. ' "All things are lawful," but not all things are beneficial. "All things are lawful," but not all things build up. Do not seek your own advantage, but that of the other' (1 Cor. 10:23–24).

In Corinth, where the majority of the church were poor and socially powerless, this call to do good and love neighbours involved a remarkable empowerment.

Through the gospel God turns all Christians (including the poor majority at Corinth) into those who can bless without looking for return. When the powerless are transformed into a blessing for their community by the grace of Christ, it provides a powerful sign of the reality of the coming kingdom.

Consider your own call, brothers and sisters: not many of you were wise by human standards, not many were powerful, not many were of noble birth. But God chose what is foolish in the world to shame the wise; God chose what is weak in the world to shame the strong; God chose what is low and despised in the world, things that are not, to reduce to nothing things that are, so that no one might boast in the presence of God.

(1 Cor. 1:26–29)

In such occasions God works through the weak to provide a sign of the coming kingdom that will last, in the midst of all the things that cannot last which are created by a powerful pagan establishment.

Imitation of Christ

Ultimately for Christians, the obligation to do good is rooted not so much in the Old Testament command to love our neighbour, as in the example of Jesus, who is the fulfilment of the Old Testament. 'Be imitators of me,' says Paul, 'as I am of Christ' (1 Cor. 11:1). ' "Other regard" is an imitation of Christ.'[19] To the Romans he wrote, 'Each of us must please our neighbour for the good purpose of building up the neighbour. For Christ did not please himself' (Rom. 15:2–3).[20]

In his public ministry Jesus brought blessing and healing almost without regard for the response (although lack of faith could hinder him). In the same way Christians are called, through the gospel, to a life of indiscriminate goodness.

It was this very indiscriminate goodness, particularly his care for the poor majority, which made Jesus so subversive. His 'upside-down' kingdom was a profound threat to those who liked things the way they were. His ministry declared time, or published the sell-by date, for both the pagan Roman world and much of first-century Judaism. Paul's ministry had the same effect.

Subverting

At the heart of Roman Corinth was a patron-client relationship (which we examined earlier). Each person's social status was reflected in the size of their following. Patrons acted as 'benefactors', providing for their 'clients' in different ways, all of which were intended to place the client under an obligation to promote their patron's interests. In Corinth you climbed the ladder of success by finding a suitably prestigious patron, while patrons grew in influence by the number and influence of their clients. By definition, the poor and powerless did not count at all, as they were of no value as clients. They were literally 'things that are not' (1 Cor. 1:28). But through the gospel, 'nobodies' become 'somebodies'. The weak and powerless become benefactors, and the chain of social obligations is replaced by the obligation to 'do good'.

Bruce Winter has shown that Paul's regular directions about people not being idle, and earning their own living, need to be understood in this client-patron context.[21] When Paul tells the Thessalonians (1 Thess. 4:11) 'to aspire to live quietly, to mind your own affairs, and to work with your hands, as we directed you', the contrast is with minding your patron's affairs while he supports you. Minding your own affairs meant attending to your own needs, rather than being made secure by someone else and using your time to promote his interests: 'so that you may behave properly toward outsiders and be dependent on no one' (4:12). Rather than being dependent on powerful social climbers, whose agendas were far from those of the kingdom of God, Christians were to work in order to be able to give, without thought of personal gain or return. Behaving properly meant a life of doing good: 'Brothers and sisters, do not be weary in doing what is right' (2 Thess. 3:13).

Paul's example

At Corinth (and Thessalonika) Paul set a powerful personal example. His engagement with society was subversive in two ways.

First, he refused to use the rhetorical tricks which were the everyday tools of popular public speakers. The style of Paul's letters show that he had a training in rhetoric, but he was loath to use it when he preached. The classic passage where he states this has often been misunderstood.

> When I came to you, brothers and sisters, I did not come proclaiming the mystery of God to you in lofty words or wisdom. For I decided to know nothing among you except Jesus Christ, and him crucified. And I came to you in weakness and in fear and in much trembling. My speech and my proclamation were not with plausible words of

wisdom, but with a demonstration of the Spirit and of power, so that your faith might rest not on human wisdom but on the power of God. (1 Cor. 2:1–5)

Paul is not saying that he does not use all his intellectual powers when he preaches the gospel. He wrote the letter to the Romans from Corinth and was clearly at the height of his intellectual powers at that time. Nor is he saying that he preaches a standard 'simple' gospel irrespective of context. He was convinced that gospel proclamation is based on some minimal essentials,[22] but both his letters and his speeches in Acts show a developed ability to communicate the gospel in a way suited to the context.

What Paul is saying is that the gospel itself does not allow him to use the local mass-media salesman's tricks when he proclaims it.

> Paul made a firm decision (1:18) not to aspire to the status of a professional rhetorician, newly arrived to market the gospel as a consumer commodity designed to please the hearers and to win their approval. Whether or not such a strategy would have been successful, the nature of the gospel of Jesus Christ excluded its being treated as a market commodity tailored to the tastes and desires of market consumers.[23]

He makes the same point in his next letter to Corinth: 'We have renounced the shameful things that one hides; we refuse to practise cunning or to falsify God's word; but by the open statement of the truth we commend ourselves to the conscience of everyone in the sight of God' (2 Cor. 4:2).

There is a second reason behind Paul's decision not to use his rhetorical training. Corinth's public speakers were part of the whole patronage system. They were the media stars of first-century Corinth. Speakers came to Corinth to get their big break by finding a patron. Then they would use their skills to promote their patron and whatever their patron wanted marketed. Just as in our society advertising is interlinked with celebrity, so it was then. And just as in our society advertising is hugely influential, but also assumed to be insincere, so it was then. If Paul had asked one of the few socially powerful Christians in Corinth to support his ministry, he would have been seen as communicating this 'new' religion as a step in developing his own career. The gospel would also have been seen as a tool to promote his patron's career. Paul dared not use the patron-client system to support his ministry. His ministry subverted that very system!

As a consequence, he and his colleagues traded as tentmakers.[24] The powerful would come to order their goods and their slaves would come to collect them. But working as an artisan would have been regarded as 'weak' in that culture. 'In a city where social climbing was a major preoccupation, Paul's deliberate stepping down in apparent social status would have been seen by many as disturbing, disgusting, and even provocative.'[25]

A patron transformed

Paul's stance was not just a matter of principle. He expected the gospel to work these social transformations. The first family to be converted in Corinth was that of Stephanas, a household which Paul had baptized personally.[26] He records the extraordinary inversion and change of lifestyle which has followed their commitment to Christ.

> Now, brothers and sisters, you know that members of the household of Stephanas were the first converts in Achaia, and they have devoted themselves to the service of the saints; I urge you to put yourselves at the service of such people, and of everyone who works and toils with them. (1 Cor. 16:15–16, italics mine)

A household which, according to normal life in Corinth, expected others to serve it and to take a client status, had made itself a servant. Only such people deserve to be trusted as leaders in the church!

The gospel subverts by transforming those who receive it into people who do good without any calculation of what they might receive in return. In other words, the gospel of grace creates disciples and communities who live a lifestyle of grace.

To sum up, 'involved distinctiveness' and 'subversive engage-ment' form one holistic strategy, identified in the light of the resurrection and the hope of the kingdom. Underlying Paul's practical counsel and direction in 1 Corinthians is a theological foundation for public discipleship, for Christian citizenship. It combines a commitment to society with a clear and prior commitment to Christ and his kingdom. Bruce Winter sums it up well: 'All able bodied members of the Christian community were to seek the welfare of others in the city, even though they might be treated as "foreigners". Eschatologically, for them "every home was a foreign land", but in terms of their social ethics, "every foreign land was their home".'[27]

The vision applied

The next chapter will begin to apply this to contemporary Western culture, but first a few observations.

Involved distinctiveness

Through their involved distinctiveness, Christians bring a special view of power to the public square: a view of power held as a stewardship to be used as a tool for service for the common good. It is not a view of power as a mark of status or a tool for self-promotion. It sees power as a tool for the empowerment of all citizens, particularly the underprivileged or marginalized. Much of the old tradition of 'public service' was rooted in the Christian tradition. If we are to see a renewal of that tradition, it must come through a renewal of public discipleship. This value cannot be created by the state, but it can be grown within the church for the benefit of the state. In the first letter to the Corinthians are hidden the seeds of a new, non-patronizing civic sphere.

Paul views powerlessness not as an inescapable trap, and certainly not as an evidence of worth, but as an offence to human dignity in the image of God. In his vision the powerless are to be empowered to be a blessing. As it was with Jesus' ministry of bringing 'good news to the poor' to bless, he expects the kingdom of God to engage society from the margins.

Paul's commitment to seeking and acting on common ground, whenever it is possible in the light of the gospel, provides a good basis for Christians to act and campaign together with others. There are many people in the UK, for example, who have no active faith, but whose values are grounded in the Christian faith, whether or not they are aware of it. There is also some common ethical ground between Christianity and the other world faiths. The acids of our consumer society eat into all faith traditions with a politically correct lack of discrimination. Local multifaith partnership may well be appropriate when there is clear, common concern.

Subversive engagement

What might be the contemporary equivalent of Corinth's self-promoting patronage culture? What should a distinctive Christian public discipleship seek to subvert? The following section will identify some candidates.

Notes

1 Helpful background to 1 Corinthians can be found in the following commentaries: Anthony Thiselton, *The First Epistle to the Corinthians*, Grand Rapids: Eerdmans; Carlisle: Paternoster, 2000; Gordon Fee, *God's Empowering Presence*, Peabody: Hendrickson, 1994; Ben Witherington III, *Conflict and Community in Corinth*, Grand Rapids: Eerdmans, 1995. See also Bruce Winter, *After Paul Left Corinth*, Grand Rapids: Eerdmans, 2001.

2 Witherington III, *Conflict and Community*, p. 8.

3 Thiselton, *First Epistle*, p. 14.

4 See 1 Cor. 1:26–29.

5 S. Mitchell, in Winter, *After Paul Left Corinth*, p. 95.

6 See also 10:23.

7 For insight on the cultural context of this and many other passages in 1 Corinthians, I am grateful for the work of Bruce W. Winter, particularly in *After Paul Left Corinth*.

8 Winter, *After Paul Left Corinth*, p. 88.

9 Ibid., p. 175.

10 David Horrell, *Solidarity and Difference*, Edinburgh: T. & T. Clark, 2005, p. 176.

11 Fee, *God's Empowering Presence*, p. 806.

12 Source unknown.

13 Fee, *God's Empowering Presence*, p. 339.

14 Ibid., p. 116.

15 Richard Hays, *The Moral Vision of the New Testament*, Edinburgh: T. & T. Clark, 1996, p. 43.

16 Horrell, *Solidarity and Difference*, p. 259.

17 Ibid., p. 162.

18 Winter, *After Paul Left Corinth*, p. 267.

19 Horrell, *Solidarity and Difference*, p. 177.

20 See also Phil. 2:1–11.

21 E.g. 2 Thess. 3:6–13.

22 See 1 Cor. 15:3ff.

23 Thiselton, *First Epistle*, p. 21.

24 See Acts 18:3.

25 Witherington III, *Conflict and Community*, p. 21.

26 'I did baptize also the household of Stephanas' (1 Cor. 1:16).

27 Bruce Winter, *Seek the Welfare of the City*, Grand Rapids: Eerdmans, 1994, p. 209.

Section Two

The Corrosion of Character

4 Citizenship undermined

As at Corinth, so today some of the social forces which shape our culture undermine community and commitment and corrode character, as much in the church as in the world. The frameworks which once helped people to develop character have been eroded. In some ways our society struggles to know what is right and wrong, but much more serious is the undermining of the capacity to do what is right consistently. How can we learn to be faithful to one another and to Christ in today's culture?

Citizenship in Britain expresses substantial concerns about the direction of social change and its impact on civic engagement.

> Changes in British society in the late twentieth and early twenty-first centuries are making the conditions for cooperative action relatively harder to achieve over time. This is because Britain is now a rapidly changing, multicultural society, with a lot of geographical mobility and diverse values. The long term changes in attitudes and behaviour are moving us in the direction of declining collective participation and weakening social norms.[1]

The report identifies a number of key factors driving this change.

1. Arguably *the market state* produces a culture of instant gratification – and this brings with it a myopia of needs – individuals want benefits now and are not prepared to wait.
2. Frequent *interaction between actors becomes more difficult* as society becomes more socially and ethnically segmented as well as geographically mobile.
3. *Common values are weakened* as class solidarity and religion decline, culture diversifies and moral relativism grows stronger.
4. *Growing inequality undermines one of the important preconditions of citizenship* – that the actors are willing to cooperate because relative equality between them means that they face common problems.[2]

Please note this explicit acknowledgment of religion as a source of common values, and of the problems caused when it declines.

The BBC report *The Soul of Britain* states:

> Slowly but surely, we British are a people in decline. We are not so happy as we were; we trust other people less, our satisfaction with home life is less; we do not feel so healthy; and confidence in our institutions has fallen. Furthermore, despite our unprecedented prosperity and the lowest unemployment figure for decades, we believe that the nation is going in the wrong direction.[3]

The next paragraph begins, 'Our belief in God has also declined.' I would like to suggest that there is a direct connection.

This chapter will address the impact of these and other elements of social change on our capacity to develop moral character. Two helpful metaphors have been used to illustrate the effect of these social forces. One is corrosion, the other the change from solid to liquid.

The corrosion of character

Character is about who we are and our capacity to behave consistently. It is about our capacity not just to know what is good or right, but to be able to do it. Character, like values, is a prerequisite of citizenship.

Any Christian perspective about destructive social trends will address the fact of human sin. The human heart lies at the centre of every society's problems.[4] Fallen human beings create fallen structures and cultural patterns – social trends, in other words. It is important to take note of social trends and also to take careful note of the scholarly analysis which identifies their causes and underlying values.

Richard Sennet's book *The Corrosion of Character*, which gives this section its name, is such a piece of scholarship. Corrosion is a powerful metaphor. Imagine an old building whose weight-bearing metal girders are rusting away and can no longer support the load they were built to bear. One of the 'girders' which sustain character is long-term committed relationships, where loyalty and trust have time to develop and be tested. For previous generations, the workplace was the primary place, outside the family, where this was experienced. Sennet studied the impact of the changing nature of work relationships on the development of character. He identified a conflict between the demand of the workplace and the demands of family and community. 'The qualities of good work are not the qualities of good character.'[5]

The shape of the workplace has changed radically. Jobs for life are becoming increasingly rare. Firms frequently restructure themselves, downsize, or outsource whole sections of their work. Many skilled people change jobs much more frequently than in the past. Un-skilled people are in danger of long-term unemployment. Retraining is a norm. A person's prospects may only be as good as his or her last assignment.

Sennet is not asking whether this is right or good for the workplace. He is pointing to the social cost. 'How can long term purposes be pursued in a short term society? How can durable social relationships be sustained?'[6] Some aspects of social change in the workplace have a destructive impact on both trust and commitment. (The technical term is 'social capital', a theme which will be addressed later in this chapter.) The loss of long-term consistent employment has contributed to the reduction in our capacity for long-term committed relationships in other dimensions of life. Sennet writes:

'No long term' is a principle which corrodes trust, loyalty and mutual commitment. Trust can, of course, be a purely formal matter, as when people agree to a business deal or rely on one another to observe the rules in a game. But usually deeper experiences of trust are more informal, as when people learn on whom they can rely when given a difficult or impossible task. Such social bonds take time to develop ... The short time frame of modern institutions limits the ripening of informal trust.[7]

Character is formed through committed relationships. The erosion of one leads to the corrosion of the other. Sennet's work is important because it is based on field research. In particular, he revisited work contexts which he had originally researched twenty years earlier. The impact of change from one generation to the next is seen clearly in his work. One manager told him, 'You can't imagine how stupid I feel when I talk to my kids about commitment. It's an abstract virtue to them; they don't see it anywhere.'[8]

The church has no instant protection from social change. If character is corroded, or never developed, it has an impact on the churches too. Sennet gives an example of this which I found very disturbing.[9] He tells of a group of hi-tech middle-aged computer programmers made redundant when an American IBM office downsized. The men went through three reactions. First they said that the company had betrayed them. Then they blamed the global economy and the Indian workers who had 'taken their jobs'. Finally they blamed themselves. This coincided with a change of behaviour in the community. Many of them had community roles. They had been the equivalent of local counsellors and school governors. But they dropped out of these responsibilities, losing interest in civic affairs. There was only one involvement which they not only maintained, but continued with greater commitment: their membership of their churches. At least one seems to have come to personal faith at this time. We must always rejoice at the conversion of anyone. It is supremely important. But it also matters what sort of Christianity and what sort of church they are converted to! Sennet's work shows that some contemporary expressions of community are a means of defence and self-protection. 'Today "we" has become an act of self-protection. The desire for community is defensive, often expressed as a rejection of outsiders.'[10] His comment on the redundant program-mers was, 'My neighbours have turned inward.'[11] Sadly these churches seem to be characterized by 'disengaged distinctiveness' rather than 'involved distinctiveness', and by 'defensive withdrawal' rather than 'subversive engagement'. Churches may have to choose between being refuges from the effects of social change and being agents of God's transformation.

Liquid society

The second metaphor that I find helpful describes our society as changing from solid to liquid. The scholar who uses this imagery is Zygmunt Bauman. Bauman has a great gift for images which make the social changes he identifies accessible to his readers. He has also described recent changes as moving from 'hardware to software'.[12] For some years Bauman used the language of modernity and postmodernity, writing a number of landmark books.[13] He became dissatisfied with the 'postmodern' vocabulary, however, believing that it failed to allow for the continuities as well as the discontinu-ities of recent cultural change. Looking around for an alternative vocabulary, he began to write of the fluid or liquid nature 'of the present, in many ways novel, phase in the history of modernity'.[14] The image is rooted in Karl Marx's statement about modernity, 'All that is solid melts into air.' But the aim of modernity was to melt some old solids and then establish some new ones. Another sociological term for this is 'disembedding', as when plants are dug up. At times of major social change, people are disembedded, but the intention, with both people and plants, is to re-embed them in new stable forms of life or community. During the Industrial Revolution many rural workers were disembedded from rural areas and work in agriculture to be re-embedded in the cities to work in factories.

Bauman says that the speed of social and technological change is now so fast that there is no time for re-embedding. The solids of society are being melted with no time for them to become solid again. In his view, 'The solids which are in the process of being melted at the present time are the bonds which interlock individual choices in collective projects and actions.'[15] In other words, this stage of modernity dissolves committed relationships.

Metaphors such as 'corrosion' and 'melting' help to illustrate the nature of the changes we are experiencing. Now we need to turn to the main factors which contribute to that change. I will identify three in the following chapters – but please note that they are interlocking, not independent of each other.

Notes

1 Charles Pattie, Patrick Seyd and Paul Whiteley, *Citizenship in Britain*, Cambridge: Cambridge University Press, 2004, p. 280.

2 Ibid., p. 280f., italics mine.

3 This BBC poll was conducted between 25 April and 7 May 2000.

4 According to Jesus, Mark 7:20–23.

5 Richard Sennet, *The Corrosion of Character*, New York: Norton, 1998, p. 21.

6 Ibid., p. 26.

7 Ibid., p. 24.

8 Ibid., p. 25.

9 Ibid., pp. 123–130.

10 Ibid., p. 138.

11 Ibid., p. 130.

12 Zygmunt Bauman, *Society Under Siege*, Cambridge: Polity Press, 2002, p. 27.

13 E.g. *Intimations of Postmodernity*, London: Routledge, 1992; and *Postmodernity and Its Discontents*, Cambridge: Polity Press, 1997.

14 Zygmunt Bauman, *Liquid Modernity*, Cambridge: Polity Press, 2000, p. 2. See also *Liquid Life*, 2005, *Liquid Love*, 2003, *Liquid Fear*, 2006, and *Liquid Times*, 2007, all from Polity Press.

15 Bauman, *Liquid Modernity*, p. 6.

5 Individualization

The ugly sociological term 'individualization' sums up the consequences of all the trends, too complex to mention here, which have resulted in what the philosopher Charles Taylor calls 'the massive subjective turn of modern culture'.[1] Taylor also writes of 'a common picture of the self as drawing its purposes, goals and life plans out of itself, seeking "relationships" only insofar as they are "fulfilling" '.[2] Like the former IBM employees mentioned earlier, people have turned inwards to find their 'real' selves within themselves, rather than through relationships and their role in society. The public world then stops being primarily a place to serve the common good, and instead becomes a means of securing personal security or identity. 'It is the private that colonizes the public space.'[3]

Individualism is now one of the core philosophical presuppositions and individualization one of the core social structures of our society. The leading German sociologist Ulrich Beck says, 'Individualization is becoming the social structure of the second modernity itself.'[4]

Social capital

In recent years, partly as a consequence of the growing trend towards individualism, a great deal of writing about society has focused around the theme of social capital. Social capital is about trust. 'Trustworthiness lubricates social life.'[5] It has been described as 'the glue which holds societies together'.[6]

Formally, social capital is about 'networks together with shared norms, values and understandings that facilitate co-operation within or among groups'.[7] It is both personal and social. Social capital is created by people meeting together regularly, for whatever reason, and the mutual and informal trust which is established as a result. It can be broken down into bonding capital, which strengthens existing communities, and bridging capital, which creates trust between different communities. Unrestrained individualization undermines it, whatever the form.

This was brought to public attention by Robert Putnam's groundbreaking book *Bowling Alone*. Writing from the United States, Putnam commented, 'Without at first noticing, we have been pulled apart from one another and from our communities over the last third of the [twentieth] century.'[8] Putnam demonstrated that social capital had declined in the US by 50% over four generations. He agreed that pressures of time and money, greater mobility and the increase in private leisure technology like the Walkman and the iPod had all contributed to the decline, but demonstrated that 50% of the decline was due to changes of attitude down the generations. 'Members of any given generation are investing as much time in organizational activity as they ever were, but each successive generation is investing less.'[9] There has been a slippage in commitment, and in belonging to organizations and clubs which require meeting face to face, deteriorating from one generation to another, for four generations. 'Generational effects means that society changes, even though individuals (within a given generation) do not.'[10] One direct consequence of this is the massive decline in membership of organizations such as trade unions, political parties and churches. Professor Grace Davie characterizes religion in Britain as 'believing without belonging'.[11]

Another direct result has been a dearth of leadership in many voluntary organizations. Scout groups, church organizations and many other voluntary groups have often been led by the same people, now quite elderly, for many years. These people keep leading for three reasons. First, this is what their generation 'do'. Second, improved healthcare has significantly increased life expectancy. Third, they cannot find anyone younger to take over! This is what Putnam means by 'society changes, even though individuals (within a given generation) do not'.

The situation in the UK is not identical to that in the US, but there are strong points of similarity and Putnam's work has been given detailed attention. The introductory article in the 2003 edition of *Social Trends* was about social capital. It stated, 'Research indicates that organisational membership and trust in other people are closely linked.'[12] *Citizenship in Britain*, published a year later, agreed and pointed out that membership was now a minority activity. 'In fact membership of organised groups is a minority activity, since 55% of Britons are not members of any group. In addition many of the 45% of people who are members of groups pay their dues and do very little else.'[13]

Social Trends showed that age has a major impact on social capital, and that 'trust in neighbours' is declining by age group.[14] Young adults aged between sixteen and twenty-nine were found to be the least neighbourly. On both sides of the Atlantic teenagers are now the age group most vulnerable to suicide. Putnam wrote:

> Our youth are in fact telling us that in their experience most people really aren't trustworthy. Perhaps thick trust – confidence in personal friends – is as strong as ever, as some Gen Xers believe. However thin trust – the tenuous bond between you and your nodding acquaintances from the coffee shop, that crucial emollient for large, complex societies like ours – is becoming rarer.[15]

Inevitably a number of other factors contribute to this decline: the increasing pace of change creates a sense of a fluid culture and of 'constantly having to live in a temporary world'.[16] The breakdown of the family is both a symptom and a cause of this decline. 'The chances that the family will survive any of its members gets slimmer by the year: the life-expectation of the individual mortal body seems an eternity by comparison.'[17] Nothing seems capable of outlasting our individual selves. 'There are few if any reference points left which could reasonably be hoped to lend a deeper and longer-lasting significance to the moments we live ... Partnerships, families, skills, places of work, neighbourhoods, possessions, styles and habits.'[18]

This has a potentially alarming impact on personal well-being. Putnam quoted the psychologist Martin Seligman:

> Individualism need not lead to depression as long as you can fall back on large institutions – religion, country, family. When you fail to reach some of your personal goals, as we all must, you can turn to these larger institutions for hope ... But in a self standing alone without the buffer of larger beliefs, helplessness and failure can all too easily become hopelessness and despair.[19]

'A self standing alone' is often seen as an ideal today, but it is a profoundly damaging one. An individualized society is also profoundly difficult to govern.

The changing nature of community

In an address to Faithworks, Tony Blair said, 'At the heart of my politics has always been the value of community, the belief that we are not merely individuals struggling in isolation from each other, but members of a community who depend on each other, who benefit from each other's help, who owe obligations to each other. From that everything stems: solidarity, social justice, equality, freedom. We are what we are, in part, because of the other.'[20] This is a view of community which is deeply coherent with the Christian faith, but far from the nature and direction of community in Britain today.

The combination of individualism and increased mobility has led to profound changes in the nature of community. There has been a substantial move from community based on neighbourhood to community through the creation of networks. This is regularly pointed out by the sociologists. 'The communities of the Global Age generally have no local centre. People living in the same street will have fleeting relationships with each other, having widely differing lifestyles and household arrangements, and have common interest only in the maintenance of certain shared facilities they take for granted.'[21] 'People do not build their meaning in local societies ... because they select their relationships on the basis of their affinities.'[22] The comments are exaggerated, but they do indicate the direction of change. 'Local' is an increasingly difficult word to define. These changes are not inherently wrong. I simply point out their contribution to the breakdown of former patterns of relationship.

Even some forms of contemporary community are a symptom of this trend. The emergence of gated communities of like-minded people, or of people on a similar – usually high – economic level, may be bonding social capital, but it is set up against bridging social capital. Communities of the like-minded are products of individualization.

When people meet less frequently, and social capital is in decline, bureaucracy becomes the fallback position for co-operation within society. Superficially, a bureaucratic society regulating an increasing proportion of everyday life would seem to be the enemy of individualizaton, but in practice it is individualization's Siamese twin. Thus the society in which we live is one in which 'bureaucracy and individualism are partners as well as antagonists'.[23] Societies with declining social capital also become increasingly litigious. 'The telling evidence of civil litigation, particularly in matters of compensation and damages, is a specific example of the more general disposition of blame, accusation and conflict in our common discourse.'[24]

All of this has substantial impact on citizenship. The pioneering French scholar Alexis de Toqueville once suggested that 'the individual is the citizen's worst enemy'.[25] In his view, the citizen is a person inclined to seek his or her own welfare through the well-being of the city, while the individual tends to be lukewarm, sceptical or wary about 'common cause' or the 'common good'. One hundred and fifty years later, the authors of *Citizenship in Britain* seemed to agree when they wrote, 'This book could have been entitled "The Atomised Citizen" since this reflects many of the trends we are observing in contemporary Britain ... There are clearly costs associated with this development.'[26] They identified an increase in 'NIMBYist politics': we need to make this provision, but 'not in my back yard'!

To many secular scholars, there is a fundamental flaw in our society. As Beck says, 'We are all asked to seek biographical solutions to systemic contradictions.'[27] In other words, individual choice alone cannot create a society where mutual trust and the common good are valued. It has to be a matter of shared conviction. Sennet warns that 'a regime which provides human beings no deep reasons to care about one another cannot long preserve its legitimacy'.[28]

Biblical reflection

It is time we returned to Scripture. Our capacity for commitment, trust and loyalty does not depend on social forces alone, but on the nature of God. The faithfulness of God is one of the foundational claims of both Old and New Testaments. In fact, the very concept of covenant (testament) is dependent on it. The God of the Scriptures is the God who keeps his promises. God's faithfulness makes human faithfulness possible and demands that we be faithful to God and to one another.[29] 'Have we not all one father? Has not one God created us? Why then are we faithless to one another?' (Mal. 2:10) 'The summons of a God who is himself faithful and able to undergird all our action is therefore the most profound resource and reason for human faithfulness.'[30]

If we return to 1 Corinthians, we are told twice that 'God is faithful' (1 Cor. 1:9; 10:13). Because he is faithful, we – those who are created in his image, and especially those who are born into his family – are also expected to be faithful (1 Cor. 4:2, 17). If human beings are made in the image of a faithful God, we have a capacity to be faithful, and we need not surrender to the corrosion of character. Further, if we are made in the image of a relational God, we have a capacity for relationships and will find our identity and can establish our character more in relationship to others than in individual freedom and a journey inwards.

The fully developed doctrine of the Trinity, which is the distinctive Christian understanding of God, was developed over several centuries. But that work only made explicit what is implicit in the New Testament. The first letter to the Corinthians has an implicit trinitarian theology. In 8:4 Paul quotes the Shema (Deut. 6:4), the central Old Testament creed, prayed three times a day by pious Jews, 'There is no God but one.' But in verse 6 he includes Jesus in the unity of the only God: 'There is one God, the Father, from whom are all things and for whom we exist, and one Lord, Jesus Christ, through whom are all things and through whom we exist.' 'Paul has quoted the most central and holy confession of Jewish monotheism and has placed Jesus firmly in the middle of it.'[31] In chapter 12, God (the Father), Jesus (the Lord) and the Holy Spirit are honoured in parallel clauses: 'No one can say "Jesus is Lord" except by the Holy Spirit. Now there are varieties of gifts, but the same Spirit; and there are varieties of services, but the same Lord; and there are varieties of activities, but it is the same God who activates all of them in everyone' (1 Cor. 12:3–6).

We are created in the image of a relational God. The divine identity is a community. So, as a consequence, is human identity. 'What is needed today is a better understanding of the person, not just as an individual, but as someone who finds his or her true being-in-communion with God and with others, the counterpart of a Trinitarian doctrine of God.'[32] Our Christian understanding of God inevitably leads us to grieve the impact of individualization. It challenges us to live an alternative to it, and to do all that we can to reverse it. It is the journey out, in relationships, not the journey into isolated selves, which is the key to fulfilment. Ultimately we are not individuals, we are persons in relationship, who need one another if we are truly to become ourselves. We have a different understanding of human flourishing, and thus a different view of human freedom.

Jürgen Moltmann beautifully sums up these implications of the doctrine of the Trinity for our understanding of human nature in these words:

> I am free and feel myself to be free when I am recognised and accepted by others and when I, for my part, recognise and accept others. I become truly free when I open my life for others and share it with them, and when others open their lives for me and share their lives with me. Then the other person is no longer a limitation on my freedom but the completion of it.[33]

Other people need not limit me; God created them to complete me. This is profoundly expressed in the Christian understanding of marriage, but it is true of God's intention for all human relationships. Our culture fears commitment, and that fear lies at the heart of the decline in social capital. Many secular authors, however, recognize that this is to our loss. As one character says to another in Tony Parsons' *Man and Wife*, 'You give up your freedom for something that's better ... It wasn't meant to make you feel trapped ... It was meant to set you free.'[34] I will conclude this section with a Christian author, and with the words of Jesus, 'We find our being only in relationships, but therein we really do find our being: "He who loses his life ... will find it."'[35]

Notes

1 Charles Taylor, *The Ethics of Authenticity*, Cambridge, Massachusetts: Harvard, 1991, p. 26.

2 Charles Taylor, *Sources of the Self*, Cambridge: Cambridge University Press, 1989, pp. 38–39.

3 Zygmunt Bauman, *Liquid Modernity*, Cambridge: Polity Press, 2000, p. 39.

4 Ulrich Beck and Elisabeth Beck-Gernsheim, *Individualization*, London: Sage, 2002, p. xxii.

5 Robert Putnam, *Bowling Alone*, New York: Touchstone, 2000, p. 21.

6 Ann Morisy, *Journeying Out*, London: Morehouse, 2004, p. 48.

7 Quoted in *Social Trends 2003*, London: TSO, 2003.

8 Putnam, *Bowling Alone*, p. 27.

9 Ibid., p. 62.

10 Ibid., p. 248.

11 Grace Davie, *Religion in Britain since 1945 – Believing Without Belonging*, Oxford: Blackwell, 1994. Professor Davie now believes that 'vicarious religion' is a more accurate description.

12 *Social Trends 2003*, p. 20.

13 Charles Pattie, Patrick Seyd and Paul Whiteley, *Citizenship in Britain*, Cambridge: Cambridge University Press, 2004, p. 265.

14 *Social Trends 2003*, p. 22.

15 Putnam, *Bowling Alone*, p. 142.

16 Richard Scace, *Britain in 2010*, Oxford: Capstone, 2000.

17 Zygmunt Bauman, *Community*, Cambridge: Polity Press, 2001, p. 47.

18 Zygmunt Bauman, *Society Under Siege*, Cambridge: Polity Press, 2002, p. 193.

19 Martin Seligman, in Putnam, *Bowling Alone*, p. 264f.

20 Tony Blair, 22 March 2005.

21 Martin Albrow, *The Global Age*, Cambridge: Polity Press, 1996, p. 156.

22 Manuel Castells, *The Internet Galaxy*, Oxford: Oxford University Press, 2001, p. 126.

23 Alasdair MacIntyre, *After Virtue*, London: Duckworth, 1981, p. 35.

24 Vernon White, *Paying Attention to People*, London: SPCK, 1996, pp. 51–52.

25 Alexis de Toqueville, quoted in Bauman, *Liquid Modernity*, p. 36.

26 Pattie et al., *Citizenship in Britain*, p. 275.

27 Ulrich Beck, *Risk Society*, London: Sage, 1992, p. 137.

28 Richard Sennet, *The Corrosion of Character*, New York: Norton, 1998, p. 148.

29 For a developed argument along these lines, see Vernon White, *Identity*, London: SCM, 2002.

30 Ibid., p. 87.

31 Tom Wright, *What St Paul Really Said*, London: Lyon, 1997, pp. 66–67.

32 James Torrance, in Alasdair Heron (ed.), *The Forgotten Trinity*, Oxford: CCBI, 1991, p. 15.

33 Jürgen Moltmann, *Humanity in God*, London: SCM, 1983, p. 64.

34 Tony Parsons, *Man and Wife*, London: BCC/CCBI, 1991, p. 281.

35 White, *Paying Attention to People*, p. 100.

6 Consumerism

If individualization creates the structure of our society, consumerism provides its dominant ideology and its navigation mechanism or satellite navigation system. Individuals navigate a multichoice world by being consumers. To at least one Christian sociologist, consumerism is the controlling partner: 'In the dynamics of our culture, consumption has now become the dominant faith and individualism, together with other subordinate commitments, serves it.'[1]

Shopping has become the basic metaphor for making our life choices. The Swedish authors of an international symposium called 'Elusive Consumption' asserted, 'Consumption and consumerism is gradually trickling into all areas of human life. It is closely related to being an individual, and is – for good or bad – the foundation of human existence.'[2] Allowing for the hyperbole, they convey clearly the extent of this change in Western society.

Citizenship in Britain also makes the connection between individualism and consumerism, and its impact on citizenship. 'This pattern of individualistic engagement makes it meaningful to talk about "consumer citizenship".'[3]

Perhaps the most significant factor in the move from modernity to postmodernity, or from solid modernity to liquid modernity, or from the first to the second modernity (the titles don't really matter), is the move from production to consumption. We have moved from a society which shaped its members primarily as producers – those who believed in progress, in producing something which contributed to the better life that was certain to come through education and hard work – to a society which shapes its members first and foremost by the need to play the role of consumer. Like all cultural shifts, it is the direction and scale of the change, not the complete replacement of one way of life with another, that matters. 'The difference is one of emphasis, but that shift does make an enormous difference to virtually every aspect of society, culture and individual life. The differences are so deep and ubiquitous that they fully justify speaking of our society as a separate and distinct kind – a consumer society.'[4] As David Lyon explains:

> Where once Westerners might have found their identity, their social togetherness and the ongoing life of their society in the area of production, these are today increasingly found through consumption. It's not that companies are producing less, or that people no longer work. Rather the meaning of these activities has altered. We are what we buy. We relate to others who consume the same way that we do. And the overarching system of capitalism is fuelled by, and geared to stimulating, consumption.[5]

This distinct kind of society, 'novel' in the opinion of some scholars,[6] has a different core value from the era preceding it. The central value of our society has moved from progress to choice: the absolute right of freedom to choose. 'Choice lies at the centre of consumerism, both as its emblem and as its core value.'[7] This is, of course, a move from a shared vision (progress) to an individual one (the sovereign consumer). 'Consumer choice is now a value in its own right.'[8] Citizenship needs to be undergirded by values, but not all values sustain citizenship.

In this society everyone becomes a consumer. The consumer society is quite simply the environment in which we live.

> The amount of money available to individuals for consumption varies enormously, but virtually everyone today is a consumer to some

degree. The poor have fewer resources than the rich, most ethnic and racial minority groups have much less to spend than members of the majority, children fewer means than adults, and so on, but all are enmeshed in the consumer culture. Even those who live on the streets survive off the discards and charity of that wildly affluent culture.[9]

The difficulty of making a Christian evaluation of consumerism is that it has to be assessed at a number of levels. At one level it is simply the cultural environment in which we live, and different from the culture in which our parents were socialized. At this level, suggesting a Christian way of life outside consumerism is like suggesting a lifestyle for fish out of water. Christian responses to consumerism, which suggest we can live apart from it, are not credible! At another level the consumer society has considerable benefits. Having more than what is needed to survive, and having wide-ranging freedom of choice, is a desirable stage for any society to reach. At this level poverty should be seen as a greater evil than consumerism. At the same time consumerism, like poverty, has a considerable capacity to lead us into temptation.

> Give me neither poverty nor riches;
>   feed me with the food that I need,
> or I shall be full, and deny you,
>   and say, 'Who is the LORD?'
> or I shall be poor, and steal,
>   and profane the name of my God.
> (Prov. 30:8–9)

Neither consumption nor shopping are wrong in themselves, but it is at the third level, where consumerism functions as an ideology, or dominant worldview, that we need to recognize it as one of our nation's primary idolatries.

An idol is a good part of the creation which is claiming much more than its due place. Like a river which has burst its banks, it needs to be put back into its proper boundaries. Within them it can be a source of good; overflowing them it can cause great damage. From this ideological perspective, and in many people's daily lives, everything becomes a consumer choice. 'Areas of social life that were previously free of the demands of the market place, including religion, have had to adapt to a world where the needs and demands of the consumer are apparently paramount ... Consumerism is arguably *the* religion of the late twentieth century.'[10] At its worst this can create a soft hedonism and a very self-indulgent society.

> Pleasure lies at the heart of consumerism. It finds in consumerism a unique champion which promises to liberate it both from its bondage to sin, duty and morality as well as its ties to faith, spirituality and redemption. Consumerism proclaims pleasure not merely as the right of every individual but also as every individual's obligation to him or her self ... The pursuit of pleasure, untarnished by guilt or shame, becomes the new image of the good life.[11]

Anyone who has never bought something because 'they owe it to themselves' or 'to make themselves feel better' should cast the first stone!

Consumerism's capacity to spread to areas well outside the marketplace is particularly evident in the way it has influenced our vocabulary for evaluating claims to truth. The language of shopping provides the vocabulary for commitment, or the lack of it.

> When many voices can be heard, who can say that one should be heeded more than another? ... When the only criteria left for choosing between them are learned in the marketplace, then truth appears as a commodity. We hear the people 'buy into' a belief or that, rather than rejecting a dogma as false, they 'cannot buy' this or that viewpoint.[12]

Claims to something objective are now frequently evaluated by subjective feelings alone, 'There being a greater desire to experience the real than to know the true.'[13] I remember a student telling me, during a mission, that he had not committed himself to Christ because 'it seems to be true, but it doesn't seem real'! As Colin Campbell says, 'A consumerist epistemology now prevails, in which "truth" is established in the same manner as the existence of wants: that is, through a scrutiny of one's internal emotional states.'[14]

One of the most serious problems which Christians should have with the impact of consumerism on daily life is with its capacity to blind us to the needs of the poor. Consumerism works as an effective economic apartheid. We do not see the ones who cannot afford to be in the shopping centre or mall. Bauman writes,

> The postmodern era is perhaps the first not to allocate a function to its poor – not a single redeeming feature which could prompt solidarity with the poor. Postmodern society produces its members first and foremost as consumers – and the poor are singularly unfit for that role; by no stretch of imagination can one hope that they would contribute to the 'consumer-led recovery'. For the first time in history the poor are totally un-functional and wholly useless; as such they are, for all practical intents and purposes, 'outside society'.[15]

The comfort of a Western consumer society makes it easy to be a spectator, almost a voyeur, on the plight of the world's poor. It becomes easy to absolve ourselves from responsibility by making a donation to a disaster relief appeal, but to have little appetite for global economic change. Given the Bible's emphasis on poverty and the poor, this should lead Christians to regard consumerist ways of life with profound suspicion. The poor are a gospel issue. Jesus identified his message as 'good news to the poor'.

We are shaped by the things to which we surrender ourselves.[16] Consumerism as a practical ideology is a character-forming practice. It can create an addictive pattern, based on the arousing and meeting of short-term needs or wants. We seem to shop as much for sensations as for actual things. Bauman comments:

> For the successful alumni of consumer training the world is an immense matrix of possibilities, of intense and ever more intense sensations, of deep and deeper still experiences ... The world and all its fragments are judged by their capacity to occasion sensations and ... to arouse desire ... more satisfying than the satisfaction itself.[17]

The move from a society committed to progress to a society committed to choice has a further consequence. At the beginning of this section I quoted *Citizenship in Britain*, which connected consumerism with the decline in conditions for acting co-operatively: 'Arguably *the market state* produces a culture of instant gratification –

and this brings with it a myopia of needs – individuals want benefits now and are not prepared to wait.' Consumer culture is a culture of instant gratification. Its dominance in our society is evidence that we have lost our hope in progress, our certainty about a better world in the future, which made it worth making sacrifices in the present. 'In the absence of long-term security, instant gratification looks enticingly like a reasonable strategy.'[18] But it is also a practice which undermines character, weakening or stunting the development of our capacity to wait, or to make sacrifices for others. 'Now, is the keyword of life strategy.'[19] Bauman warns, 'The rise of the consumer is the fall of the citizen.'[20]

The metaphysics of consumerism

The cultural history which had led to this dominant role of consumerism was amusingly summed up by Jean Baudrillard in a fable. 'Once upon a time there was a Man who lived in Scarcity. After many adventures and a long journey through Economic Science, he met the Affluent Society. They married and had lots of needs.'[21] It is a mistake, however, to regard consumer culture as a materialist culture. Alan Hirsch, an Australian missiologist and former advertising professional, says, 'I have little doubt that in consumerism we are now dealing with a very significant religious phenomenon. If the role of religion is to offer a sense of identity, purpose, meaning and community, then it can be said that consumerism fulfils all these criteria.'[22] Consumerism has a spirituality. One critic described the free market as 'this consoling replacement for the divinity'.[23]

Two scholars, Colin Campbell, professor of sociology at the University of York (mentioned earlier), and the American Roman Catholic scholar Vincent Miller, have provided me with the most convincing explanation of the power of consumerism in our culture. In his paper 'I Shop Therefore I Know That I Am: The Metaphysical Basis of Modern Consumerism', Campbell asks, 'Why has consuming come to occupy such a central place in our lives',[24] when this has not been the case in former years? He also identifies the 'unrestrained individualism of consumer culture'.[25] Like Bauman, who once described postmodernity as being like 'a shopping mall overflowing with goods whose major use is the joy of purchasing them',[26] Campbell recognizes that the heart of consumerism does not lie in the things we own or wish to own. 'The real location of our identity lies in our reaction to products, not in the products themselves.'[27] Bauman speaks of sensations, Campbell of desire. 'It is the processes of wanting and desiring that lie at the heart of the phenomenon of modern consumerism.'[28] Miller also agrees that 'desire is fundamental to consumer culture'.[29]

Campbell identifies the inner subjective nature of consumer desire. 'Wants can only be identified subjectively ... Modern consumerism is more to do with feeling and emotion (in the form of desire) than about reason and calculation.'[30] He comments on the close link between personal tastes and personal identity. In personal adverts, when seeking a partner, many people describe their identity through what they enjoy: 'Thirty-five-year-old man into line dancing and karate looking for ... ' and so on. Campbell says, 'That is where we are most likely to feel that our uniqueness as individuals – our individuality actually lies.'[31] He then identifies two typical (if rather dated) expressions, 'there is no disputing tastes' and 'the customer is always right', and comments, 'I would suggest that the assumptions embodied in these two sayings – that there is no disputing tastes and that the customer is always right – have become the basis for a widespread and largely taken-for-granted individualist epistemology, one in which the "self" is the only authority in matters of truth.'[32] But the heart of consumer spirituality is not found in the individual as their own authority, but in the need of each 'soul standing alone' to be assured about their identity and significance. For Campbell, the key to the power of consumerism is found in 'the deeper underlying human need for reassurance concerning the reality of the self'.[33] In other words, consumer choice provides an assurance mechanism about individual authenticity and worth. I am told to buy male anti-ageing cream 'because I'm worth it'.

If this is right, then consumerism actually provides a counterfeit of Christian assurance – an assurance mechanism which competes with the work of the Holy Spirit as a guarantee of my personal significance and promise of the future. The Christian experience of the assurance of salvation is rooted objectively in what Christ has done and in the written witness of Scripture. It is evidenced in a new capacity for committed relationships.[34] But the subjective element consists of the inner witness of the Holy Spirit.[35] In the New Testament the Spirit is understood and experienced as the fore-taste or first instalment of the power which will one day transform the universe.[36] In Christian spirituality the Spirit is experienced as the guarantee and promise that the faithful God will fulfil his promises and complete all that he has begun in Christ.

Consumer spirituality provides a parallel and alternative: each consumer 'satisfaction' confirming the consumer's sense of his or her own authenticity, and each identified desire renewing the promise of happiness. The heart of consumerism is not products, but the process through which we desire and consume them.

Campbell believes that the marketplace has drawn this from the New Age. 'We can discern in the New Age worldview all those elements of a consumerist metaphysic.'[37] I believe the truth may be the other way round. Consumerism has one of two effects. For the majority, it provides a counterfeit assurance which makes authentic spirituality seem unnecessary. For a minority, it creates a consumer-shaped religion, of which the New Age is typical. The parallels with Christian spirituality are closer than those of the New Age. As Miller's work makes clear, 'Consumer culture poses a particularly vexing problem for Christianity because the shape and texture of the desires that it cultivates are profoundly similar to Christian forms of desire.'[38] He sees consumerism as a way of life which forms our character. Consumer desire is 'a system of formation that structures desire in a manner similar enough to Christianity to sidetrack it in subtle but profound ways'.[39] Here is a powerful counterfeit: similar enough to Christianity, but subtly sidetracking it.

Miller identifies two complementary processes in consumer character-building: seduction and misdirection.

Seduction is not really about the seductive qualities of particular products, but the ongoing process that keeps us moving on from one consumer choice to another. 'Seduction concerns our relationship to objects of desire. Contrary to what is generally assumed, consumer desire is not focused on particular objects, but is instead stretched out across an endless series of potential objects.' It provides a consumer hope, a consumer promise of the future. 'Consumer desire is not focused on particular things; it is constantly enticed to go beyond what has been acquired to consider something new.'[40] 'Seduction spurs consumption by prolonging desire and channelling its inevitable disappointments into further desires.'[41] Consumer desire is made up of a chain of wanting, being satisfied (or not) and becoming dissatisfied, often through the development of a new desire. In this way, disappointment does not make well-trained consumers suspicious of the process, but functions as a source of energy to identify new needs. 'Seduction uses the surplus of dissatisfaction as a spur to encourage only more consumption.'[42]

Miller shows the close parallels (as well as the profound differences) this has with the Christian desire for God. Augustine wrote, 'You made us for yourself and our hearts find no peace until they rest in you.' Miller comments, 'Consumer desire mimics the restlessness of our earthly pilgrimage.'[43] This is a very different character formation from that created by the Holy Spirit. The Spirit strengthens our capacity for love and commitment. Consumer formation undermines our capacity 'to sustain commitment beyond the moment of choice'.[44] In reality, a consumer lifestyle can become a series of experiences of broken promises. But there is always another desire!

Misdirection services the idolatrous element of consumerism. Misdirection is 'the advertising strategy of associating commodities with needs, desires and values that are not directly related to the given products. Misdirection works by encouraging consumers to fulfil more profound needs and desires through consumption.'[45] We are all used to adverts whose attractive primary images bear absolutely no rational connection to the product being advertised. The subliminal suggestion is that consuming the product is the gateway to greater things. 'He can't be a man, because he doesn't smoke the same cigarettes as me!'

Campbell describes consumerism as 'a kind of default philosophy for all of modern life'.[46]

> The fact that consuming has acquired a central significance in our lives could indicate something very different from the common suggestion that we are all victims of selfish materialism and acquisitiveness ... Consumerism should no longer be viewed as a desperate and necessarily futile response to the experience of meaninglessness, but rather as the very solution to that experience.[47]

From a Christian perspective, consumerism provides a counterfeit solution. It reinforces individualism, undermines commitment, forms addictive patterns and provides false assurance. Its primary impact in our society is to offer an experience which makes religion seem unnecessary. For a minority, including some in the church, it turns spirituality into a consumer experience, enjoyed for its own sake, but with no desire for transcendence or transformation. Habits form character. The consumer habit, left unchallenged, cannot form Christian character.

David Lyon was right to observe that 'the everyday challenge of consumerism has yet to be fully acknowledged by most Christian communities'.[48]

Biblical reflection

Two themes in 1 Corinthians are of obvious relevance: idolatry and concern for the poor.

Os Guinness wrote a story about a man stealing wheelbarrows from a shipyard. Every day his barrow was searched and nothing found. But all along he was stealing the barrows. Os told the story to illustrate the dangers of the culture of modernity which were in front of our faces, but so much a part of everyday life that we failed to see them or appreciate the dangers to the church. The same applies to consumerism.

Something similar is seen in the concerns about idolatry in 1 Corinthians. Many in the Corinthian church were converts from idolatry (12:2). Paul challenged them to resist any temptation to return to the worship of idols (10:7, 14). He told them that the stories of the Old Testament were written for their benefit, so they could be sure that they would not be tempted beyond their strength, but would be provided with the way out in any time of temptation. The pressing discipleship issue which concerned them was whether or not it was permissible to eat meat which had been offered to idols (chapters 8 and 10). But some of them were treating this issue way out of proportion. They would never eat in a non-Christian's house in case they were offered meat from a temple. They were so keen to maintain distinctiveness that they lost all involvement with their neighbours. Others treated the issue too lightly. They engaged in all social activities with their fellow citizens with no element of gospel subversion. Paul gives advice which would maintain both involved distinctiveness and subversive engagement.

There was, however, another idolatry, the idolatry of social power and status, embodied in the patronage system, which many in Corinth failed to recognize as an idol at all. It is the Corinthian equivalent of the wheelbarrow that nobody notices, because they are focused on something inside it. It is this that Paul challenges by example and by apostolic exhortation. If the idolatry that the Corinthians overlooked was patronage, for today's church it is consumerism. We must take it seriously.

The Corinthian church, like the Western one today, was tempted to ignore the poor, even in their own congregations.

> For, to begin with, when you come together as a church, I hear that there are divisions among you; and to some extent I believe it ...
> When you come together, it is not really to eat the Lord's supper. For when the time comes to eat, each of you goes ahead with your own supper, and one goes hungry and another becomes drunk. What! Do you not have homes to eat and drink in? Or do you show contempt for the church of God and humiliate those who have nothing? What should I say to you? Should I commend you? In this matter I do not commend you!
> (1 Cor. 11:18–22)

The poor are always a gospel issue. The good news of God's grace to sinners is also good news to the poor. We are not permitted to make choices between Romans 3 – 5 and Luke 4, or between Paul and James. We need forgiveness for our sins of omission as well as for our sins of commission. We need forgiveness for injustice as well as for pride. In Christ we are reconciled to one another through being reconciled to God. In fact, the idol of status, as embodied in the patronage system, was the root of the wealthier Corinthian Christians' lack of concern for their poorer brothers and sisters. Without 'involved distinctiveness' and 'subversive engagement', whether engaging patronage or consumerism, even the church's worship is compromised.

Notes

1 Alan Storkey, in Craig Bartholemew and Thorston Moritz (eds.), *Christ and Consumerism*, Carlisle: Paternoster, 2000, p. 100.

2 Karin M. Ekstrom and Helene Brembeck, *Elusive Consumption*, Oxford: Berg, 2004, pp. 1–2.

3 Charles Pattie, Patrick Seyd and Paul Whiteley, *Citizenship in Britain*, Cambridge: Cambridge University Press, 2004, p. 267.

4 Zygmunt Bauman, *Work, Consumerism and the New Poor*, Buckingham: Open University, 1998, p. 24.

5 David Lyon, 'Memory and the Millennium', in T. Bradshaw (ed.), *Grace and Truth in the Secular Age*, Grand Rapids: Eerdmans, 1998, p. 284.

6 E.g. Anthony Giddens, *Modernity and Self-Identity*, Cambridge: Polity Press, 1991, p. 199.

7 Yiannis Gabriel and Tim Lang, *The Unmanageable Consumer*, London: Sage, 1995, p. 27.

8 Zygmunt Bauman, *Liquid Modernity*, Cambridge: Polity Press, 2000, p. 87.

9 George Ritzer, *Enchanting a Disenchanted World*, London: Pine Forge, 1999, p. 36.

10 Steven Miles, *Consumerism as a Way of Life*, London: Sage, 1998, p. 1.

11 Gabriel and Lang, *The Unmanageable Consumer*, p. 100.

12 Lyon, 'Memory and the Millennium', p. 285.

13 Colin Campbell, 'I Shop Therefore I Know That I Am: The Metaphysical Basis of Modern Consumerism', in Ekstrom and Brembeck, *Elusive Consumption*, p. 35.

14 Ibid., p. 34.

15 Zygmunt Bauman, in Dennis Smith, *Zygmunt Bauman – Prophet of Postmodernity*, Cambridge: Polity Press, 1999, p. 193.

16 See Rom. 6:16.

17 Bauman, *Work, Consumerism and the New Poor*, p. 32.

18 Bauman, *Liquid Modernity*, p. 162.

19 Ibid., p. 163.

20 Zygmunt Bauman and Keith Tester, *Conversations with Zygmunt Bauman*, Cambridge: Polity Press, 2001, p. 114.

21 Jean Baudrillard, *The Consumer Society*, London: Sage, 1998, p. 69.

22 Alan Hirsch, *The Forgotten Ways*, Grand Rapids: Brazos, 2006, p. 107.

23 Frederic Jameson, *Postmodernism of the Cultural Logic of Late Capitalism*, London: Verso, p. 273.

24 Campbell, 'I Shop Therefore I Know That I Am', p. 27.

25 Ibid., p. 28.

26 Zygmunt Bauman, *Intimations of Postmodernity*, London: Routledge, 1992, p. vii.

27 Campbell, 'I Shop Therefore I Know That I Am', p. 32.

28 Ibid., p. 28.

29 Vincent Miller, *Consuming Religion*, London; New York: Continuum, 2004, p. 116.

30 Campbell, 'I Shop Therefore I Know That I Am', p. 29.

31 Ibid., p. 31.

32 Ibid., p. 33f.

33 Ibid., p. 35.

34 See 1 John 3:10–14.

35 See Rom. 8:15f.

36 The Spirit is the first fruits of the harvest which will be reaped at the end of the age (Rom. 8:23). He is the down payment, the first part of what will be received in full when Christ returns (2 Cor. 1:22; 5:5; Eph. 1:14). He is the seal which guarantees 'the day of redemption' (2 Cor. 1:21–22; Eph. 1:13; 4:30). He is the present dynamic power of the future age (Heb. 6:4, 5; Acts 1:8; 1 Cor. 4:4).

37 Campbell, 'I Shop Therefore I Know That I Am', p. 39.

38 Miller, *Consuming Religion*, p. 107.

39 Ibid.

40 Ibid., p. 141.

41 Ibid., p. 109.

42 Ibid., p. 130.

43 Ibid.

44 Ibid., p. 145.

45 Ibid., p. 109.

46 Campbell, 'I Shop Therefore I Know That I Am', p. 42.

47 Ibid.

48 David Lyon, *Jesus in Disneyland*, Cambridge: Polity Press, 2000, p. 145.

7 Constructivism

Closely entwined with individualization and consumerism is constructivism. This is the conviction that truth, identity and so on are not givens, waiting to be discovered, but interpretations 'made up' in different circumstances.[1] This is not merely a significant intellectual trend, but a practical way of viewing and inhabiting the world. It is the controlling story of the liquid modern era. As David Lyon observes, 'Identities are constructed through consuming. Forget the idea that who we are is given by God or achieved through hard work in a calling or a career: we shape our malleable image by what we buy – our clothing, our kitchens, and our cars tell the story of who we are (becoming).'[2]

All cultures have an underlying story, which they tell themselves about themselves. Each culture operates out of a worldview and the foundation of that worldview is a story, which leads to and results in a way of life.[3] Worldviews are about presuppositions. They are 'like the foundations of a house: vital but invisible. They are that *through* which, not *at* which, a society or an individual normally looks; they form the grid according to which humans organize reality, not bits of reality that offer themselves for organization. They are not usually called up to consciousness or discussion ... '[4]

During the last decades, our culture has changed its story. We used to have a story about scientific and technological progress, a story about making the world better. Now we have a constructivist story, a story about making ourselves up through our individual choices. Without questioning or thinking about it, contemporary Westerners seem to see themselves as 'beings in an endless process of becoming'.[5] Humans are assumed to be self-generating. 'A notion is presented ... that self-creation is an endless possibility.'[6]

All of this seems self-evident, because it is continually socially reinforced. Our advert-soaked consumer culture seems to say to us, 'Do whatever you want to do and be whatever you want to be.' 'Just do it!' say Nike. 'It's an on-demand world. Respond faster, stay ahead,' say IBM. 'Reinvent yourself today, tomorrow may be too late,' says an advert for a new novel displayed in London Underground stations. But this is not just a marketing message. An overview of sociological studies on young people's experience of life in the UK concluded that for contemporary young people, 'everything is presented as a possibility'.[7] These authors call this aspect of our society, and the way it shapes its young citizens, an 'epistemological fallacy'. This is sociological jargon for an untruth. The options open to the more affluent Westerners are indeed extraordinary, by comparison with other economic groups and other periods of history. Character is indeed formed by the way we exercise our choices. But individual choices are not the primary source of identity, and we are not individual free agents, unrestrained by social forces.

Unchallenged at the heart of our contemporary cultural story lies a theory of constructivism. Human identity and understandings of truth are not given or revealed, but socially constructed. If the ideological opponent of the church in modernity was secularism, constructivism fills that role in its liquid form. And like all effective heresies, it is partly right. Humans are made in God's image to be culture-builders, and their sense of identity is built up in that activity. But if the assumption of God is withdrawn from the equation, human beings see themselves as entirely self-generating, within only the social and economic constraints of their particular context.

This means that the sharing of the gospel in such a context will involve 'the stumbling block of creation' long before it reaches the stumbling block of the cross. As one theologian warns us, 'It is the distinction of the human creature, created in the image of God, to be called to exercise its created destiny in *finite* freedom . . . Where it interprets itself as absolute self-created freedom and denies its character as gift, it falls into a bondage from which it can find no escape.'[8]

When Christians engage with contemporary culture, they immediately, and understandably, turn to issues of truth. I will address this later in the chapter, but most secular writing, on the other hand, engages with the issue of human identity. In a consumer culture, identity is constructed through 'lifestyle', that is consumer, choices. David Lyon writes,

> Image and style are now central to identity. Nike running shoes, Levi jeans, Coca-Cola – these and more – all help to give shape to who we are. This is different from binding our identity to work or employment . . . and it raises shopping skills to the level of virtue. Likewise our social circle, our peer group, is likely to share consuming patterns in common, more than anything else.[9]

Anthony Giddens comments, 'Lifestyle choice is increasingly important in the constitution of self-identity and daily activity.'[10]

There is little room for the notion of a stable self in this perception. 'Self image through consumption is self-fuelling; it can keep you busy all your life because there is always more to buy, because if your identity is about being cool then definitions of cool are constantly changing.'[11] Communities also remain in permanent flux in areas of culture where this constructivist story goes unchallenged. Scholars talk of 'temporary tribes' and a 'nomadic' lifestyle, of 'the symbolic gathering around brand-names such as Nike, Apple Macintosh, Nintendo, Calvin Klein and so on, where consumers recognize their tribal status but retain an essentially nomadic existence'.[12] The sociological use of 'nomad' is revealing. Traditional nomadic peoples follow their lifestyle in tribes and clans. They pitch camp and move on together. But consumerism and constructivism are individualistic. We form 'temporary tribes' around common interests and then move on.

Combined with the mobility that globalization allows, this enables an experience of the self which is little more than role play. I can be one person where I work, another where I play, another where I shop, another where I commit adultery, another where I live (or sleep) and, if I go to church, another person there. This is already a significant dimension of youth culture. Role-play selves also involve the easy letting go of previous commitments.

> Changing identity may be a private affair, but it always includes cutting off certain bonds and cancelling certain obligations: those on the receiving end are seldom consulted, let alone given the chance to exercise free choice. The mobility and the flexibility of identification which characterizes the 'shopping around' type of life are mixed blessings.[13]

This is an unstable experience of the self, one on which some thrive, but from which others suffer. Some retreat from the pressures of multiple choice or of changing to stay 'cool'. They have been called 'minimal selves'. 'The self contracts to a defensive core ... emotional equilibrium demands a minimal self,' marked by 'selective apathy, emotional disengagement from others, renunciation of the past and the future, a determination to live one day at a time'.[14] David Lyon has called the consumer-constructed form of identity 'the plastic self'. He recognizes that, as in any generation, it is not the only life strategy available and identifies two other alternatives: 'the expressive self', with a focus on therapy and discovering the 'real me who can feel good about myself', and the 'subsumed self', where loss of certainty is compensated for by surrender to some authoritative group, whether religious, ethnic or formed around some single issue.[15]

Not everyone is happy in a constructivist world. Some thrive, some find alternative coping mechanisms. Few challenge the underlying story. It is assumed that 'the aesthetic life is the ethically good life'.[16] Whatever feels good to me must be good. It is also assumed that 'identity comes from the outside, not the inside. It is something we put or try on, not something we reveal or discover.'[17] But things we try on can be discarded just as quickly. Stable identity does not sit easily with a constructivist lifestyle.

At the heart of all this is a profound ambiguity about the self. The self must be solid enough to feel like 'me', but flexible enough to keep changing in new circumstances. As David Lyon points out, 'The self is both central and fragmented.'[18] It is central, because in an individualist society it alone has the right to choose. It is fragmented, because there is no stable me, but an ongoing multichoice exercise. If my identity is created by my consumer choice, then who is the 'me' who chooses what to choose?

Zygmunt Bauman perceptively pointed out that liquid modern culture is marked not so much by the construction of identity as by the evasion of accountability. 'The hub of postmodern life strategy is not identity building but avoidance of fixation.'[19] Keep the options open. The constructivist way of life is simply the twenty-first-century formulation of human sin. I refuse accountability to anyone other than myself. In this chapter, I have focused on the impact of these social forces and philosophical assumptions on citizenship and the public square. But their deeper explanation is theological. The loss of God leads to the crisis of identity. If there is no created identity to discover, then I have little alternative but to make myself up.

It should not, then, surprise us that one contemporary understanding of truth is also constructivist. Again the nomadic theme appears. 'We all become nomads, migrating across a system that is too vast to be our own, but in which we are fully involved, translating and transforming bits and elements into local instances of sense.'[20] If there is no revealed truth, no truth out there, then consumerism provides me with a coping vehicle, for some accompanied with a great sense of freedom and liberation. I pick and mix my own truth.

For some writers, that is all that has ever been possible. In his defence of *The Satanic Verses*, Salman Rushdie wrote:

> Human beings do not perceive things whole; we are not gods but wounded creatures, cracked lenses, capable only of fractured perceptions. Partial beings, in all the senses of that phrase. Meaning is a shaky edifice we build out of scraps, dogmas, childhood injuries, newspaper articles, old films, small victories, people hated, people loved; perhaps it is because our sense of what is the case is constructed out of such inadequate materials that we defend it so seriously, even to the death.[21]

This also has a theological explanation. The American philosopher Richard Rorty wrote, 'The suggestion that truth, as well as the world, is out there is a legacy of an age in which the world was seen as the creation of a being who had a language of his own.'[22] Christians believe in a Creator God who is also a speaking God. In the light of God, truth and identity are revealed realities to be discovered and inhabited. Rorty looks for a day when we are 'no longer able to see any use for the notion that finite, mortal, contingently existing human beings might derive the meaning of their lives, from anything except other finite, mortal, contingently existing human beings'.[23] But we derive our meaning from, and serve, the God who created and redeemed the world through his only begotten Son, who is his incarnate Word to every human society.

Biblical reflection

Paul, of course, assumes that truth is rooted in the reality of God. He assumes that there is a God who speaks and acts – not a philosopher's God (whether Plato or Rorty), but a God who reveals himself by acting in history. This God has acted throughout the history of Israel, and what he did has been written in the old covenant Scriptures.[24] These writings, fulfilled in Christ,[25] give reliable guidance for life for those who belong to the new covenant. 'These things happened to them to serve as an example, and they were written down to instruct us, on whom the ends of the ages have come' (1 Cor. 10:11).

In fulfilment of those Scriptures, God has ultimately and finally acted in Christ. 'For I handed on to you as of first importance what I in turn had received: that Christ died for our sins in accordance with the scriptures, and that he was buried, and that he was raised on the third day in accordance with the scriptures' (1 Cor. 15:3–4). The incarnation, death and resurrection of Christ are the central point of human history. They are the place to stand if we want to see life as it really is.

Human philosophy, or wisdom as Paul calls it, can never grasp this. 'Where is the one who is wise? Where is the scribe? Where is the debater of this age? Has not God made foolish the wisdom of the world? For since, in the wisdom of God, the world did not know God through wisdom, God decided, through the foolishness of our proclamation, to save those who believe' (1 Cor. 1:20–21). Wisdom is found in Christ.

> For Jews demand signs and Greeks desire wisdom, but we proclaim Christ crucified, a stumbling block to Jews and foolishness to Gentiles, but to those who are the called, both Jews and Greeks, Christ the power of God and the wisdom of God. For God's foolishness is wiser than human wisdom, and God's weakness is stronger than human strength … He is the source of your life in Christ Jesus, who became for us wisdom from God, and righteousness and sanctification and redemption.
>
> (1 Cor. 1:22–25, 30)

Christian faith does not depend on human wisdom, because that wisdom will fail. It depends on the power of God through the work of Christ.[26]

Some contemporary human wisdom or philosophy assumes that belief in God is an arrogant claim to a 'God's-eye view of the world', that we claim to have some sort of spectators' gallery onto the universe, which gives us 20/20 vision about life, the universe and everything. But the spectators' gallery view of truth is not a Christian one. Christians do not claim to have total truth. 'We know only in part' (1 Cor. 13:9). They claim to have sufficient truth to receive God's salvation and to live life faithfully for him, in the light of the future he has promised. 'Now I know only in part; then I will know fully, even as I have been fully known' (1 Cor. 13:12). Only God is omniscient. Christians claim to know the God who knows and saves them.

The spectators' gallery view of truth is an Enlightenment one which has been seriously undermined by more recent thinkers. They rightly claim that it is not possible for us to 'leap out of our conceptual schemes, our social practices, our skins, or whatever, to gain a more veridical (certain) view of the world'.[27] All knowledge is perspectival; we can only see from where we stand, from the perspective we take. All humans have some capacity to transcend themselves and their viewpoint, but we have no access to a spectators' gallery. However, to acknowledge that human knowing is perspectival is not to say that it is all relative, that no one can claim that their truth is the truth. The thing about perspectives is that how much you can see depends on where you stand. When I lived in York, I could stand outside my church and see a little of the ancient city wall. But if I crossed the road and made the effort to climb to the top of York Minster's tower, on a clear day I could see halfway to Hull on the coast. It all depends where you stand.

Christians believe that we do not have to step outside our skins to be sure of truth. We believe that God in Christ stepped into our skins. We believe that to see through the eyes of the incarnate Son of God is to see the world as its Maker intends us to see it. 'In order to obtain a God's-eye view of the world, we merely need to hold true the narratives which identify Jesus (the Bible) and organize the rest of our beliefs accordingly.'[28]

In Christ, through the Scriptures, by the Spirit, Christians believe they are given access to God's ancient wisdom.

> Yet among the mature we do speak wisdom, though it is not a
> wisdom of this age or of the rulers of this age, who are doomed to
> perish. But we speak God's wisdom, secret and hidden, which God
> decreed before the ages for our glory ... these things God has revealed
> to us through the Spirit; for the Spirit searches everything, even the
> depths of God.
> (1 Cor. 2:6–7, 10)

Christians cannot accept a fully constructivist view of truth. We are constructivists under licence, stewards working with the sufficient truth and knowledge that God has given us. We do not make up our own truth; we live God's truth as disciples and citizens.

Notes

1 For an introduction, see Kenneth Gergen, *An Invitation to Social Construction*, London: Sage, 1999.

2 David Lyon, *Jesus in Disneyland*, Cambridge: Polity Press, 2000, p. 12.

3 For a detailed description of this understanding of worldviews, written from a Christian perspective, see N. T. Wright, *The New Testament and the People of God*, London: SPCK, 1992, pp. 122–126.

4   Ibid., p. 125.

5   Colin Campbell, 'I Shop Therefore I Know That I Am: The Metaphysical Basis of Modern Consumerism', in Karin M. Ekstrom and Helene Brembeck, *Elusive Consumption*, Oxford: Berg, 2004, p. 37.

6   Kieran Flanagan, *The Enchantment of Sociology*, Basingstoke: Macmillan, 1996, p. 32.

7   Andy Furlong and Fred Cartmel, *Young People and Social Change*, Buckingham: Open University, 1997, p. 7.

8   Christoph Schwöbel, 'God, Creation and the Christian Community', in Colin Gunton (ed.), *The Doctrine of Creation*, Edinburgh: T. & T. Clark, 1991, p. 167f.

9   David Lyon, 'Memory and the Millennium', in T. Bradshaw (ed.), *Grace and Truth in the Secular Age*, Grand Rapids: Eerdmans, 1998, p. 284.

10 Anthony Giddens, *Modernity and Self-Identity*, Cambridge: Polity Press, 1991, p. 5.

11 Madeleine Bunting, in the *Guardian*.

12 Chris Rojek, *Decentering Leisure*, London: Sage, 1995, pp. 151–152.

13 Zygmunt Bauman, *Liquid Modernity*, Cambridge: Polity Press, 2000, p. 90.

14 Christopher Lasch, *The Minimal Self*, New York: Norton, 1984, pp. 1, 58.

15 Lyon, *Jesus in Disneyland*, pp. 91–95.

16 Mike Featherstone, *Consumer Culture and Postmodernism*, London: Sage, 1991, p. 126.

17 Simon Frith, *Performing Rites*, Oxford: Oxford University Press, 1996, p. 273f.

18 Lyon, *Jesus in Disneyland*, p. 69.

19 Zygmunt Bauman, *Life in Fragments*, Oxford: Blackwell, 1995, p. 89.

20 Iain Chambers, 'Cities Without Maps', in Job Bird, Barry Curtis, Tim Putnam, George Roberton and Lisa Tickner (eds.), *Mapping the Futures*, London: Routledge, 1993, p. 193.

21 Salman Rushdie, *Imaginary Homelands*, London: Granta, 1991, p. 12.

22 Richard Rorty, *Contingency, Irony and Solidarity*, Cambridge: Cambridge University Press, 1989, p. 4f.

23 Ibid., p. 45.

24 See 1 Cor. 1:19, 31; 3:19; 9:9, 10; 10:7; 14:21; 15:45, 54.

25 See 1 Cor. 10:1–4.

26 See 1 Cor. 2:5.

27 Bruce D. Marshall, *Trinity and Truth*, Cambridge: Cambridge University Press, 2000, p. 169.

28 Ibid.

8 Today's young people (Generation Y)

The three elements interlocked

This may all seem very theoretical, but it translates into a way of life. If individualization creates the structure of our liquid modern society, consumerism is its navigation mechanism and constructivism its controlling story, we would expect to see significant evidence of this among young people in particular. Recent research on Generation Y (15–25-year-olds), with which I was involved, provides that confirmation.[1]

The significance of Generation Y rather than Generation X was that this was the first generation of British young people who had only known the liquid modern culture. (Generation X was a hinge generation, experiencing both the old and new modernities in conflict.) The research identified a coherent worldview which we called 'the happy midi narrative'. It was self-evident to these young people that the purpose of life was to be happy. They regarded the world in which they lived as meaningful in itself, and saw no need to think of finding their significance anywhere else. They also saw the world as essentially benign. Although difficult things do happen in life, there are enough resources within the individual and his or her family and friends to enable happiness to prevail.

It is important to note that the research was done with socially included young people, because they are the majority. Socially excluded young people are likely to see the world differently. For the young people in the research, life was seen as a level playing field. It was basically OK. If things went badly, then family and friends would always be there to support you. It was also assumed that if everyone was allowed to be themselves, this would add up to collective happiness.

The happy midi narrative was individualist, because friends and family were there to ensure 'my' happiness. It was consumerist, because the world of consumer choices was integral to the society which all the young people took for granted and saw as benign. It was constructivist, because this lay at the heart of allowing people to be themselves.

We called this a midi narrative because it did not take the whole of reality into account. It was an 'enough for me to get by' narrative, not a 'meaning of life' narrative. In effect, this was not so much a worldview as a pair of blinkers, allowing only certain aspects of reality to be seen. Life and reality are made to appear smaller than they really are. The individual family and friends are seen to be the only necessary resource. There was also a naïve trust in family and friends, which seemed completely unaware of the level of marriage breakdown, child and domestic abuse, and the decline in social capital, let alone aware that the individualism being celebrated was a primary factor in the decline of the very relationships which it assumed would always be there.

The young people were very positive and hopeful, but there was a shortening of hope as it has been understood by previous genera-tions. The happy midi narrative forgoes a vision of a better future together, for a better, short-term, future for ourselves as indi-viduals or families. The sociologists' 'epistemological fallacy' where 'everything is presented as a possibility' had been embraced without question.

I have no wish to condemn these young people. It is not unreasonable to want to be happy and positive and to value family and friends. Their worldview has powerful social support and seems self-evident to them. But it will not equip them to be citizens, beyond 'consumer citizenship' and NIMBY politics. Beck's comment, quoted earlier, that our society requires us 'to seek biographical solutions to systemic contradictions' is exemplified among these young people. They were identifying their biographical solutions, their hopes for their personal happiness. But their happy midi narrative has little to offer to the 'systemic contradictions' within our society, which progressively undermine the public square.

Paul describes the 'god of this world' as blinding minds.[2] The happy midi narrative appears to be an effective contemporary form of that blindfold.

Biblical reflection

It is important that Christians respond to this society in a positive rather than a negative way. As we shall see in the final section of this book, it is no Christian response to try to return to 'the good old days'. We are to live as an anticipation of God's future, not as curators of our society's past. The future will include much that has been valued in the past, but we cannot and should not attempt to return to a former society. Putnam, who sees the church as a vital resource for addressing the problems he has identified, tells us that 'the challenge for us is not to grieve over social change but to guide it'.[3]

Some of the change I have described is generational. Despite the inadequacy of their midi narrative, Generation Y thrives on uncertainty and risk. It has known only this society and has not been equipped with the analytical tools to critique it. But with good national policies and effective local communities, it can be helped towards new forms of social capital.

Nevertheless, the challenge is great. How do we grow Christians who can be public disciples, living the life of the future in advance, in this culture which, as we have seen, has the capacity to corrode both the public or civic sphere and public discipleship? Where do you grow both 'involved distinctiveness' and 'subversive engagement'? God has only one answer. It is called the church. By way of preparation for the next part of the book, I will conclude this section with a last visit to 1 Corinthians, in particular to chapter 12.

Just as Paul used the church as a temple as an image of an alternative society, so he used the image of the body. Our difficulty is that we have become far too familiar with the image of the church as the body of Christ. We have used it in debates about spiritual gifts, and as a way of understanding the internal life of the church, but have often missed its force. Paul was quite capable of coining new language to express the new reality called the church of Jesus Christ, but his use of the term 'body' was well established in Greek and Roman culture. Livy, Seneca, Plutarch and Epictetus all used it as a metaphor for society, and Paul follows their usage down to the details. In a famous play, Livy places it on the lips of a Senator Menenius, who uses his eloquence to persuade the plebeians, who have gone on strike, to return to work. He does this by arguing that if the active members or limbs (the plebeians) fail to feed the belly (the pares, or governing classes), the whole body will die. In other words, in Greco-Roman culture the body metaphor is used in a high-status argument for each to have their proper place. Hierarchy is regarded as natural. The body metaphor is a device at the service of patronage.

Paul utilizes it by turning it upside down (a nice example of subversive engagement). 'Paul here questions rather than utilises the "natural" hierarchy.'[4] He writes:

> On the contrary, the members of the body that seem to be weaker are indispensable, and those members of the body that we think less honourable we clothe with greater honour, and our less respectable members are treated with greater respect; whereas our more respectable members do not need this. But God has so arranged the body, giving the greater honour to the inferior member, that there may be no dissension within the body, but the members may have the same care for one another. If one member suffers, all suffer together with it; if one member is honoured, all rejoice together with it. Now you are the body of Christ and individually members of it.
> (1 Cor. 12:22–27)

Only this is Christ's way – 'so it is with Christ' (12:12). It is the way of life which results from baptism (v. 13), it is the way his lordship is expressed among his people (v. 3) and it is God's arrangement (v. 24) to ensure equality and mutual care (v. 25). The result is 'a form of solidarity constructed through reversing the conventional positions of high and low, wise and foolish, honourable and dishonourable, and fostering instead a mutual and egalitarian other-regard'.[5]

We must note that then as now, the way of life Paul describes is neither self-evident nor easy for Christian disciples. As with many other themes in his letters, Paul addresses this theme to a church manifestly failing to be the sort of church he describes. Then as now, powerful social forces pulled the local church the opposite way. But Paul assumes that by the grace of the Holy Spirit Christians can live this way. The way of life that he describes is the way of life that our society, as described in this chapter, requires.

Here is a community that is committed to both bonding and bridging social capital; a community that is not just of the like-minded or all from the same social group. 'To build bridging social capital requires that we transcend our social and political and professional identities to connect with people unlike ourselves.'[6] Here also is a community that seeks to embody Christ and continue his ministry in its community. Here is a Christian community in which 'edification', the building up of others, is the purpose of its internal relationships (1 Cor. 14), but also the purpose of its relationships with non-believers. Here also is a community where character is cultivated.

If the Christian community is to bear witness to the life of the future in the present, then its way of life is meant to show the whole of society God's healthy form of living. If we want public disciples, we will have to give attention to the nature of our churches, in the light of Scripture.

Notes

1 Sara Savage, Sylvia Collins-Mayo, Bob Mayo and Graham Cray, *Making Sense of Generation Y*, London: Church House Publishing, 2006. See also Bob Mayo, *Ambiguous Evangelism*, London: SPCK, 2004.

2 See 2 Cor. 4:4.

3 Robert Putnam, *Bowling Alone*, New York: Touchstone, 2000, p. 402.

4 David Horrell, *Solidarity and Difference*, Edinburgh: T. & T. Clark, 2005, p. 123.

5 Ibid., p. 124.

6 Putnam, *Bowling Alone*, p. 411.

Section Three

The Cultivation of Character

9 Character

When character is corroded, involved distinctiveness loses its distinctiveness, and subversive engagement stops being subversive. Or, as Jesus put it, 'if the salt has lost its taste ... it is no longer good for anything'. And the lamp is under the basket.[1] The local church is central in developing Christ-like character in its members, in order to model God's healthy alternative way of living. If we want public discipleship, we will need disciple-making churches. If we want to resist the corrosion of character in our churches, then we will need to learn how to cultivate character. A vision for public discipleship will not suffice. It will only be a wistful hope, without the local capacity to embody it consistently.

What is character?

We need to return to the subject of character. In this context, I do not mean individuality or distinctiveness, as in 'he's such a character'. Rather I mean the capacity to act consistently, regularly doing what is believed to be right, despite pressures (external or internal) to the contrary. Character frees me to act consistently according to what I believe. As we shall see, a Christian understanding of freedom has much more to do with being free for what is right than with being free from things which limit my choice. Stanley Hauerwas describes freedom as 'a quality that derives from having a well formed character'.[2]

Used in this sense, character can be linked to virtue, to integrity and to a more profound understanding of identity than that used in consumer culture. It is not automatic or instant, despite our culture's love of instant everything, but is acquired over time. It is linked to identity because it involves the capacity to develop a consistent understanding of the self and maintain a coherent personal story.[3] 'What strengthens the sense of identity are those things which require a person to be continuous with who he or she was.'[4] This may sound very theoretical, but one practical example is keeping a promise. To keep a promise requires you, in that area at least, to act consistently with the person you were when you made it. Character exists 'when one becomes deeply and habitually disposed to respond' consistently.[5] How we behave when we are caught off guard, in moments of crisis, or when we are under pressure will largely be decided by the habits and patterns of life which we have formed over time. We act out of the character we have developed. What we have been in the past shapes how we will perform in the present. The Duke of Wellington is alleged to have said, 'The battle of Waterloo was won on the playing fields of Eton.'[6]

For Christians, character development is also about God's mercy and forgiveness. If our characters have become more like Christ over the years, then we have been recipients of God's grace.

> We attain character not by our constant effort to reach an ideal, but by discovery, as we look back on our lives, and by God's forgiveness, claim them as our own. Character, in other words, names the continuity of our lives, the recognition ... that our lives are not just the sum of what we have done, but rather are constituted by what God has done for us.[7]

How is character formed?

1. By the choices we make

Character is formed by the choices we make, in particular by the habits we form, for good or ill. Paul was particularly clear about this.

> Do not be deceived; God is not mocked, for you reap whatever you sow. If you sow to your own flesh, you will reap corruption from the flesh; but if you sow to the Spirit, you will reap eternal life from the Spirit. So let us not grow weary in doing what is right, for we will reap at harvest time, if we do not give up.
> (Gal. 6:7–9)

Archbishop Rowan Williams once preached at the national memorial to the Victoria Cross. He spoke about bravery as 'second nature'. He warned that people for whom bravery is instinctive, or their first nature, can put their own lives, as well as those of their companions, foolishly at risk. But true bravery is found in those who acknowledge and overcome their fear and tendency for self-preservation and then put their lives at risk for the sake of others. This is bravery as 'second nature'. The archbishop went on to ask how such bravery is developed. He spoke of 'a time to look at how our daily decisions lead us towards or away from such virtue, towards a point where we have grown to be the sort of people for whom it is unthinkable not to act selflessly and honourably'.[8] It is our daily decisions which lead us towards or away from Christian character and the possibility of public discipleship.

This is a particular challenge in a consumer culture, the foundational value of which is my right to choose what suits me. 'Modern consumerism is, by its very nature, predominantly concerned with the gratification of wants rather than the meeting of needs.'[9] Consumerism is addictive and encourages a self-centred 'first nature' rather than the development of a 'second nature' concerned for others. Indirectly it discourages thoughtful reflection about the needs of others. 'Modern consumerism is more to do with feeling and emotion (in the form of desire) than about reason and calculation, whilst it is fiercely individualistic, rather than communal in nature.'[10]

My choices form my character. A consumer culture fosters the illusion that I remain infinitely free to choose – but any choice limits my choices. As Archbishop Williams writes:

> I am changed by my choices, and I can't simply revert to the position I had before – which is itself a position already defined and limited by choices. Real choice both expresses and curtails freedom – or rather it should lead us further and further away from a picture of choice that presupposes a blank will looking out at a bundle of options like goods on a supermarket shelf.[11]

In practice, every selfish choice, made without thoughtful reflection, makes it more likely that I will choose selfishly the next time. Choices really do limit freedom as much as they express it. They form character.

2. Through a community whose story we share

Despite the power of contemporary individualism, we are all also shaped by the communities to which we belong, even if those communities seem little more than temporary consumer tribes. We are likely to choose the way the people around us choose. And we are likely to choose to associate with people we think will choose like us. Superficially, an individualistic society would be likely to be one marked by diversity and full of distinctive personalities. In practice, a consumer society tends to be a conformist one. We appear to have unimaginable choice, but the choice is of infinite minor variety within a very narrow way of life.

According to the sociology of knowledge, our view of life, and thus the way we make choices, is closely related to the context in which we live.[12] The technical term is 'plausibility structures'. The cultural context in which we live makes certain views of life, and thus certain choices, seem obvious or plausible. 'We seldom live by ideas or ideologies but rather by images of life communicated by our surrounding worlds.'[13] 'The power of any culture is measured by the extent to which its formulation of reality seems "natural".'[14] 'Ideas and world views are maintained by social support. They are culturally embedded in community.'[15]

How this works is demonstrated clearly in two well-known films.

In *The Matrix*, humans exist in a virtual world (the Matrix), created and controlled by artificial intelligence, but they experience their lives as though they were free. When Neo, the lead character, begins to question his reality, he is told by the leader of the resistance, 'The Matrix is everywhere, it's all around us, here even in this room. You can see it out your window, or on your television. You feel it when you go to work, or go to church or pay your taxes. It is the world that has been pulled over your eyes to blind you from the truth.' The Matrix made humans take their perception of reality for granted.

In *The Truman Show*, the lead character has lived his whole life within a huge dome, in which an artificial world has been created. He does not know that he is the subject of a non-stop TV reality show. He is in his thirties before he catches on and questions his reality. When the director of the show is asked why it has taken so long for Truman to work it out, he replies, 'We accept the reality of the world with which we are presented. It's as simple as that!' It is as simple as that. Cultures provide an appropriate stability to life. They should make our choices plausible or implausible. But we should always maintain our ability to question our culture's interpretation of its reality.

Paul sees culture as a blindfold, keeping people from seeing their need of Christ. 'In their case the god of this world has blinded the minds of the unbelievers, to keep them from seeing the light of the gospel of the glory of Christ, who is the image of God' (2 Cor. 4:4). By 'the world' he means culture organized apart from the Creator. It is this which the devil uses to 'blind minds'. In other words, culture can provide a false plausibility for our choices, and stifle questions we should be asking. David Runcorn wrote, 'The ultimate question at the heart of choosing is not what we wish to acquire, but what kind of world we are seeking to be a part of.'[16]

If Christian character is to be formed by the choices we make in a consumer culture, we will need to practise an alternative plausibility. Plausible ways of life are rarely questioned, unless they fail to deliver what they promise. Consumerism works because, although it is based on a series of short-term promises, it delivers to many people the comfortable life for which they are looking. If, however, people see and experience a valid, and potentially superior, alternative, they are much more likely to question their current way of life. This applies to each Christian learning to live distinctively and to the church's corporate witness to society.

As Andrew Walker says, 'If the world staggers onwards with more consumption, wrapped up in mass culture yet splitting at the seams, we will need to create sectarian plausibility structures in order for our story to take hold of our congregations and root them in the gospel.'[17] By 'sectarian' he does not mean separate from society, he means involved distinctiveness: salt that remains salty.

Christian character is formed by the making of consistent choices, within a community of faith, where there is mutual encouragement to live a distinctively Christian life. But what characteristics are needed for Christian citizens?

Notes

1 See Matt. 5:13.

2 Stanley Hauerwas, *The Peaceable Kingdom*, London: SCM, 1983, p. 37.

3 Anthony Giddens, *Modernity and Self-Identity*, Cambridge: Polity Press, 1991, p. 54.

4 David Wells, *Losing Our Virtue*, Leicester: IVP, 1998, p. 144.

5 R. C. Roberts, 'Character', in *New Dictionary of Christian Ethics and Pastoral Theology*, Leicester: IVP, 1995.

6 See Samuel Wells, *Improvisation: The Drama of Christian Ethics*, London: SPCK, 2004, p. 78f.

7 Stanley Hauerwas and Charles Pinches, *Christians among the Virtues: Theological Conversations with Ancient and Modern Ethics*, Notre Dame, Indiana: University of Notre Dame, 1991.

8 Rowan Williams, sermon at the national memorial to the Victoria Cross, 14 May 2003.

9 Colin Campbell, 'I Shop Therefore I Know That I Am: The Metaphysical Basis of Modern Consumerism', in Karin M. Ekstrom and Helene Brembeck, *Elusive Consumption*, Oxford: Berg, 2004, p. 28.

10 Ibid., p. 29.

11 Rowan Williams, *Lost Icons*, Edinburgh: T. & T. Clark, 2000, p. 32.

12 See the work of Peter Berger.

13 Michael Paul Gallagher, *Clashing Symbols*, London: Darton, Longman and Todd, 1997, p. 4f.

14 James Hunter, 'What is Modernity?', in Philip Sampson, Vinay Samuel and Chris Sugden (eds.), *Faith and Modernity*, Oxford: Regnum, 1994, p. 13.

15 Andrew Walker, *Telling the Story*, London: SPCK, 1996, p. 124.

16 David Runcorn, *Choice Desire and the Will of God*, London: SPCK, 2003, p. 70.

17 Walker, *Telling the Story*, p. 190.

10 Character for citizenship

Both our nations and the kingdom of God need citizens with a vision of the public good, combined with a willingness for self-sacrifice – people who will act for and support the common good when they might not benefit themselves. We need citizens who are as committed to fulfil their obligations as to insist on their rights. We need Christians who will live their faith in public, as the primary way to seeking the well-being of others. We have to develop 'the habits needed for a full life of joyful responsibility with and for others before God'.[1] This combination is both distinctive and demanding.

Knowing and doing what is right

If character is cultivated through consistent choices, two things are needed: to know what is right, and to have the capacity to do what we know is right.

Knowing what is right

Our culture seems full of agonizing moral dilemmas, as technology advances. Christian citizens will need a good grounding in biblical ethics as new dilemmas arise. They will also need to be clear about the moral frameworks which Scripture provides.

Paul wrote his letters as a devout member of the old covenant community who had discovered the Messiah and the new covenant. As he led his mission to the Gentiles, he had to be clear which pieces of old covenant legislation were fulfilled in Christ and no longer operative, such as the sacrificial system based in the temple (which was still operational throughout his lifetime). He also had to distinguish between practices which were once the boundary markers of the people of God (like food laws and circumcision) but which were now just Jewish cultural practices, and lasting moral commandments for the whole people of God.

His letters identify a cluster of principles for ethical living in the new covenant. At the heart of these is the holiness of God. God has revealed himself as holy. Because he is holy, we, his people, are to be holy.[2] To this end he has given us his Holy Spirit.

> For this is the will of God, your sanctification: that you abstain from fornication; that each one of you know how to control your own body in holiness and honour, not with lustful passion, like the Gentiles who do not know God; that no one wrong or exploit a brother or sister in this matter, because the Lord is an avenger in all these things, just as we have already told you beforehand and solemnly warned you. For God did not call us to impurity but in holiness. Therefore whoever rejects this rejects not human authority but God, who also gives his Holy Spirit to you.
> (1 Thess. 4:3–8)

Daily bodily life is to be holy, because the Creator and Redeemer is holy. Those made in the image of God are to reflect God in their daily lives. In Christ the broken image is being restored. 'Ethics for Paul is ultimately a theological issue pure and simple – that is, an issue related to *the known character of God*.'[3]

For Paul, the will of God has also been revealed in his commandments. In the new covenant he made a clear distinction between cultural practice and moral obedience. 'Circumcision is nothing, and uncircumcision is nothing; but obeying the commandments of God is everything' (1 Cor. 7:19). In this text he makes a clear distinction between what is now cultural and what is abiding morality.

Following the teaching of Jesus, he saw the love of neighbour as fulfilling the essence of God's commandments, as they applied to our human relationships.

> Owe no one anything, except to love one another; for the one who loves another has fulfilled the law. The commandments, 'You shall not commit adultery; You shall not murder; You shall not steal; You shall not covet'; and any other commandment, are summed up in this word, 'Love your neighbour as yourself.' Love does no wrong to a neighbour; therefore, love is the fulfilling of the law.
> (Rom. 13:8–10; see also Gal. 5:14)

This leaves no possibility of a discipleship which withdraws from society and ignores people's needs. Public discipleship clearly involves the practical loving of neighbours – remembering that in the parable of the Good Samaritan, Jesus stretched the definition of neighbour way beyond the comfortable or the customary.

For Paul, all of this is rooted in the example of Christ himself. 'We who are strong ought to put up with the failings of the weak, and not to please ourselves. Each of us must please our neighbour for the good purpose of building up the neighbour. For Christ did not please himself' (Rom. 15:1–3). Paul refers to the death of Christ, not just as God's once-for-all means of atonement, but as a model for life in the world, for public discipleship.[4] 'Agape (love) finds its definitive expression for Paul in the figure of the pre-existent Son of God who gave himself up for us on the cross.'[5] As a consequence, Paul longs for Christ to take shape within his churches: 'My little children, for whom I am again in the pain of childbirth until Christ is formed in you' (Gal. 4:19). 'What would Jesus do?' really is a good question! But 'How may Jesus be formed in me?' is an even better one. As we shall see, 'How may Jesus be formed in us?' is better still.

This framework, in which the revealed character of God and his commandments provides the continuity, and the example of Christ the focus, provides the basis of Christian ethics. What is right is discerned in this way. In addition, of course, there is a whole variety of specific pieces of ethical instruction in the New Testament, but they all fit within this framework.[6] Everything else is 'indifferent', either cultural or leaving room for disagreement. 'Only those matters which have to do with God and his character are regarded as absolute; all others are nonessentials.'[7] But even in disagreement, Christians are not free to please themselves, if to do so would cause someone else to stumble. The example of Christ is the controlling principle here also.[8]

Christians are given clear instruction about what is right in many aspects of life, and a framework for discernment, so that we can embody the life of Christ in public. Knowing what is right is not the chief problem. Mark Twain is alleged to have said, 'It's not the parts of the Bible I don't understand which worry me, but the parts I do understand.' Knowing what is right is not the main problem. Consistently *doing* what is right is much more of a challenge.

Doing what is right

The Old Testament people of God knew what was right. They had been given God's law. But they failed to live it out, because the power of sin in their life was greater than their best aspirations to obey God. The problem with the 'good and holy law' was that sin and death work through it. The law was 'weak' through the flesh (Rom. 8:3). The problem was not the inadequacy of the law as a moral code, but its inability to empower. It could tell us what to do, but not empower us to do it.

Paul describes this in Romans 7. 'So I find it to be a law that when I want to do what is good, evil lies close at hand. For I delight in the law of God in my inmost self, but I see in my members another law at war with the law of my mind, making me captive to the law of sin that dwells in my members' (Rom. 7:21–23). It is hugely tempting for Christians to empathize with this whole passage:

> I do not understand my own actions. For I do not do what I want,
> but I do the very thing I hate ... I can will what is right, but I cannot
> do it. For I do not do the good I want, but the evil I do not want is
> what I do. Now if I do what I do not want, it is no longer I that do it,
> but sin that dwells within me.
>
> So I find it to be a law that when I want to do what is good, evil
> lies close at hand. For I delight in the law of God in my inmost self,

but I see in my members another law at war with the law of my mind, making me captive to the law of sin that dwells in my members.

(Rom. 7:15, 18–23)

But this is not Paul's description of Christian experience! It is his summary of the condition from which we are released, through Christ and by the Spirit. The passage ends with this cry, 'Wretched man that I am! Who will rescue me from this body of death?' and with this response, 'Thanks be to God, through Jesus Christ our Lord.' In chapter 6, Paul has already promised that through baptism into Christ's death believers are 'set free from sin' and need no longer allow it to 'exercise dominion in [their] bodies, to make [them] obey their passions'. Rather, he says, 'present your members as slaves to righteousness [to what is right] for sanctification'. Christians are expected to know what is right, and to do it.

Christian citizenship is rooted in the transforming power of the gospel. Sin lies at the heart of the problem of character. The gospel provides the power for transformed lives. In 1 Corinthians, Paul lists ways of life which cannot inherit the kingdom of God. At the close of the list he says, 'And this is what some of you used to be. But you were washed, you were sanctified, you were justified in the name of the Lord Jesus Christ and in the Spirit of our God' (1 Cor. 6:9–11). Through the work of Christ and the Spirit, dishonesty, sexual sin, lifestyles of excess or disrespect can change. It happened in Corinth, which remained far from a perfect church, and it can happen today.

Secular theories about human identity, like the constructivist one referred to in Section Two of this book, do not take the power of sin seriously, and cannot lead to Christian character or shape the citizens we need.

This is magnificently expressed by Miroslav Volf in his book *Exclusion and Embrace*, which is directly relevant to the question of citizenship. Volf is a Croatian theologian who teaches in the US. He gave a lecture in Germany on the theology of reconciliation, which was attended by the great German theologian Jürgen Moltmann. Moltmann asked one question, 'Can you love the Chetnik?', meaning the Serb. This was soon after a time when large numbers of Croatians had been massacred by the Serbs. Volf gave a very honest reply: 'I know I should, but I don't know if I can.' He knew what was right. Jesus taught us to love and forgive our enemies. The problem was doing it.

Exclusion and Embrace arose out of Moltmann's question and Volf's search for a reply with which he could live. En route, he addresses a variety of modern and postmodern understandings of what it means to be human. One of the theories he challenges is the constructivist one, particularly as expressed in the work of Richard Rorty. Rorty claimed that our selves have no true or given centre and that human identity is something we weave together, to give our lives the appearance of having meaning.[9] Volf, with his painful experience of recent Balkan history, uses Paul to take Rorty to task.

> Paul presumes a centred self, more precisely a *wrongly* centred self that needs to be decentred by being nailed to the cross: 'I have been crucified with Christ' (Gal. 2:19–20). Though the self may lack an 'objective' and 'immovable' centre, *the self is never without a centre*; it is always engaging in the production of its own centre. 'Weaving' (Rorty) would be a rather innocent way to describe this production ... 'Struggle' and 'Violence' come closer to being an adequate description.[10]

In effect, Volf says that it is all right for ivory-tower Western philosophers to suggest that we shop for identity and make ourselves up. In much of the world, that simply leaves you at the mercy of the most powerful, with no hope of transformation. Only the cross can transform the violent aggressor into a minister of reconciliation. Volf quotes Paul, because that was Paul's own testimony. 'For I am the least of the apostles, unfit to be called an apostle, because I persecuted the church of God. But by the grace of God I am what I am, and his grace toward me has not been in vain' (1 Cor. 15:9–10; see also Acts 22:3–16). Volf then points to the power of Christian conversion.

> Whichever way the centering takes place and whatever its result, the self should be de-centred, claims Paul ... then a recentering of that same self can take place ... The centre is Jesus Christ crucified and resurrected who has become part and parcel of the very structure of the self ... At the centre of the (new) self lies self-giving love.[11]

An encounter with the cross is intended to result in lifestyle change. Christians are to live a new Christ-centred life. That life is characterized by self-giving love, the quality most needed for citizenship. Christian freedom is not freedom from everything which might limit our choices. It is freedom from sin for the sake of service. It is not the life of licence, which so many call freedom today.

> For you were called to freedom, brothers and sisters; only do not use your freedom as an opportunity for self-indulgence, but through love become slaves to one another. For the whole law is summed up in a single commandment, 'You shall love your neighbour as yourself.' If, however, you bite and devour one another, take care that you are not consumed by one another.
> Live by the Spirit, I say, and do not gratify the desires of the flesh. (Gal. 5:13–16)

Freedom is *for* holiness and sacrificial love. As we have seen, it is born in encounter with the cross, but it is also empowered by the Holy Spirit. 'The just requirement of the law [is] fulfilled in us, who walk ... according to the Spirit' (Rom. 8:4). The just, or righteous, requirement of God's law remains as God's righteous requirement. We are to love our neighbour. This requirement could not be fulfilled by a command alone, but it can be fulfilled by the Holy Spirit at work in our lives.

Walking by the Spirit

The Hebraic worldview of both Old and New Testaments has an integrated understanding of what it means to be human. By very definition, the Holy Spirit engages the whole of our lives.[12] In both Old and New Testaments, to do is to know, and to know God is to do justice and love.[13] The Holy Spirit is the great integrator in a culture which still splits knowing from doing. When Paul contrasts the Spirit with the flesh, he is not setting the spiritual over against the physical. Nor is he comparing one part of us with another. He is talking about the Spirit as the presence and power of the age which has come in Christ and will fully come when he returns. When he talks about the flesh, he does not mean our bodies, but our whole lives lived apart from God. Primarily he means the power of the age which is passing away. The contrast is between the future world and the past one, in a time of overlap. Set free from the control of the old age, we may now live in the power of the new.

This emphasis on the Holy Spirit as the power of God's future in advance is one of the primary ways in which the New Testament speaks about the Spirit. The Spirit is the first fruits of the harvest which will be reaped at the end of the age (Rom. 8:23). He is the down payment, the first part of what will be received in full when Christ returns (2 Cor. 1:22; 5:5; Eph. 1:14). He is the seal which guarantees 'the day of redemption' (2 Cor. 1:21–22; Eph. 1:13; 4:30). He is the present dynamic power of the future age (Heb. 6:4, 5; Acts 1:8; 1 Cor. 4:4).

Jesus taught us to pray that God's will should be done on earth as it is in heaven. The Spirit comes as the answer to that prayer. 'We are brought to life by the Spirit so as to live the life of heaven on earth.'[14] Daily obedience is empowered by the Spirit, and Christian character (the fruit of the Spirit) is formed in us through that daily obedience. Paul calls this 'walking by the Spirit' as opposed to gratifying the desires of the flesh. In both Old and New Testaments, ethics is about public discipleship, about 'walking' in the ways of God. Walking is Paul's most frequent expression when writing about ethical behaviour. The tense is continuous – 'go on walking in the Spirit'. Inevitably, to walk requires continually putting one foot in front of the other. Growth in Christian character comes through an active, ongoing co-operation with the Spirit. It is what Eugene Peterson has called 'the long obedience in the same direction'. As Peterson's colleague, Gordon Fee, says,

> Life in the Spirit is not passive submission to the Spirit to do a supernatural work in one's life; rather it requires conscious effort, so that the indwelling Spirit may accomplish his ends in one's life. If such a person is also described as being 'led by the Spirit', that does not mean passively; it means to rise up and follow the Spirit by walking in obedience to the Spirit's desire ... Since the Spirit is God's own empowering presence, Paul expected God's supernatural aid to enable them to live in keeping with God's character and purposes.[15]

The command to walk by the Spirit is accompanied by a promise: 'and you will not gratify the desires of the sinful nature'. Some translations turn this into a further command: 'Do not gratify the desires of the flesh.' While this is equally possible grammatically, it does not seem to me to fit the context. Paul is saying that if we live our lives independently of Christ and the Spirit, we run the risk of being drawn into a life of licence, 'doing what you want', which he regards as a form of slavery: slavery to sin.[16] The promise is that those who continually walk by the Spirit, by saying 'yes' to God, will find that their desires and habits change. They no longer fulfil the desires of the flesh, but develop the fruit of the Spirit. 'Live by the Spirit and *you will not* gratify the desires of the flesh.' The Spirit's presence prevents you from 'doing whatever you wish'. The Spirit enables us to resist the desires of the flesh.

> The fruit of the Spirit is love, joy, peace, patience, kindness, generosity, faithfulness, gentleness, and self-control. There is no law against such things. And those who belong to Christ Jesus have crucified the flesh with its passions and desires. If we live by the Spirit, let us also be guided by the Spirit.
> (Gal. 5:22–26)

For Paul, the key issue in discipleship is the development of character. This is why he gives such emphasis to the Spirit, rather than just listing Christian duties. 'His concern is for the fundamental direction of a person's life.'[17]

Encounter with cross and Spirit

To sum up, Christian character is formed by encounter with the cross and the Spirit. 'And those who belong to Christ Jesus have crucified the flesh with its passions and desires. If we live by the Spirit, let us also be guided by the Spirit' (Gal. 5:24–25). 'The possibility for obedience ... rests on the twin facts (1) that the "flesh", which belongs to the old order, has been crucified in Christ Jesus, and (2) that present life this side of that crucifixion is empowered by the Spirit.'[18]

We cannot walk alone

Up until this point, Paul's teaching could be taken as an individualist's charter. But Paul assumes a community context, as his next few sentences in Galatians show.

> Let us not become conceited, competing against one another, envying one another.
>
> My friends, if anyone is detected in a transgression, you who have received the Spirit should restore such a one in a spirit of gentleness. Take care that you yourselves are not tempted. Bear one another's burdens, and in this way you will fulfil the law of Christ.
>
> (Gal. 5:26 – 6:2)

Westerners tend to see everything from an individualistic perspective and interpret accordingly. This is not the case in much of the world, and was certainly not the case in the first century. 'The concern from beginning to end is with Christian life in community, not with the interior life of the individual Christian ... "The fruit of the Spirit" engenders "love, joy, and peace" within the community, not primarily within the believer's own heart (5:22).'[19] It only takes a moment to see that love, joy, peace, patience, kindness, generosity, faithfulness, gentleness and self-control are relational qualities. Love is shown to someone; self-control is usually needed because others need to participate, and so on. Paul intends that both the world and, above all, the local church be the crucible in which Christian character is matured.

Within the Christian community, this finds expression in loving service. 'For you were called to freedom, brothers and sisters; only do not use your freedom as an opportunity for self-indulgence, but through love become slaves to one another' (Gal. 5:13). Christians are 'slaves to one another' rather than slaves to the law (5:1, 18). They are 'slaves to one another' through love (5:13b–14) rather than slaves to the flesh who 'bite and devour one another' (5:15). When a brother or sister sins, it is the responsibility of the community to 'restore such a one in a spirit of gentleness. Take care that you yourselves are not tempted' (6:1). Here is a concern for one another which is profoundly aware of our frailty and potential for stumbling, or even for walking in the wrong direction. Paul describes a community where the group does not take over its members' responsibility for their lives, but by mutual concern bears 'one another's burdens' and enables each to take responsibility and to walk by the Spirit. 'All must carry their own loads' (6:5).

This is never just for the church's benefit. It is not community for community's sake. It is to equip and sustain each local church for its ministry of public discipleship. Within a few verses, Paul says, 'So let us not grow weary in doing what is right, for we will reap at harvest time, if we do not give up. So then, whenever we have an opportunity, let us work for the good of all ... ' (6:9–10). Paul sees the local church as the community where the members develop an instinctive outgoing goodness. 'For in Christ Jesus ... the only thing that counts is *faith working through love*' (5:6, my italics). And all of this is available through the grace of Jesus Christ. 'The abundance of God means that the grace and energy to be virtuous are always available.'[20]

Notes

1 David Ford, *The Shape of Living*, London: Darton, Longman and Todd, 1998, p. 56.

2 See Lev. 19:2.

3 Gordon Fee, *Paul, The Spirit and the People of God*, London: Hodder & Stoughton, 1996, p. 105, italics mine.

4 E.g. concerning marriage, Eph. 5:5, 25; concerning patience, Rom. 15:1–3, etc.

5 Richard Hays, 'Christology and Ethics in Galatians', *Catholic Biblical Quarterly*, vol. 49, 1987, p. 274.

6 E.g. Paul's teaching about homosexuality in Rom. 1 is rooted in his understanding of God's character as revealed in Gen. 1 – 3.

7 Fee, *Paul*, p. 104.

8 See Rom. 14:1 – 15:6; 1 Cor. 8.

9 'If there is no centre to the self, then there are only different ways of weaving new candidates for belief into antecedently existing webs of belief and desire', Richard Rorty, *Contingency, Irony and Solidarity*, Cambridge: Cambridge University Press, 1989, p. 83f.

10 Miroslav Volf, *Exclusion and Embrace*, Oxford: Abingdon, 1996, p. 69.

11 Ibid., p. 70f.

12 In Rom. 8:5–17, the Spirit engages with our minds, bodies and hearts.

13 E.g. see Jer. 22:15–16 and 1 John 4:8.

14 Fee, *Paul*, p. 97.

15 Gordon Fee, *God's Empowering Presence*, Peabody: Hendrickson, 1994, p. 433.

16 See Rom. 6:15–19.

17 John Barclay, *Obeying the Truth*, Edinburgh: T. & T. Clark, 1988, p. 231.

18 Fee, *God's Empowering Presence*, p. 456.

19 Gordon Fee, exact source unknown.

20 Ford, *The Shape of Living*, p. 55.

'There is an intimate connection between morality and faith, and between both of these and the moral communities that foster and sustain them.'[1] Public discipleship is not an incidental responsibility of the church. It is its calling. Local churches are designed by God to be crucibles of discipleship. They are communities for Christlikeness, placed throughout the world, so that Christ may be seen and his transforming power known in every place.

'And he has put all things under his feet and has made him the head over all things for the church, which is his body, the fullness of him who fills all in all' (Eph. 1:22–23). In the letter to Ephesus, Paul spells out the cosmic role of the church in God's purposes. Fullness or completeness is found in Christ. The church is called to embody Christ, to bear his transforming completeness to every nook and cranny of creation, in anticipation of the new creation which is promised. Paul's use of the language of 'completion' makes it clear that he is not thinking of creation ending, but of creation being transformed.

In the Sermon on the Mount, Jesus teaches that distinctive Christian discipleship is for the sake of the world.

You are the salt of the earth; but if salt has lost its taste, how can its saltiness be restored? It is no longer good for anything, but is thrown out and trampled under foot.

　　You are the light of the world. A city built on a hill cannot be hid. No one after lighting a lamp puts it under the bushel basket, but on the lampstand, and it gives light to all in the house. In the same way, let your light shine before others, so that they may see your good works and give glory to your Father in heaven.

(Matt. 5:13–16)

He tells his disciples what they are, not what they ought to be. As disciples they *are* salt and light. They can lose their saltiness and hide their light, but as his disciples they are the salt and light the world needs. This means that Christians do not so much *go* to church, they *are* church. And church is for Christ's purposes in the world. Salt is an individual metaphor. Salt is scattered, speaking of the health-giving influence of the Christian community when it is dispersed in daily life. Light is a corporate metaphor, referring to the church gathered as a visibly distinctive community. Jesus links the picture of a lamp lighting a house with that of a city, like Jerusalem, set on a hill. In Old Testament understanding, Jerusalem, or Zion, was the joy of all the earth (Ps. 48:2). It was the place from which God's beauty shone out (Ps. 50:2). It was where God's king reigned as his 'son' (Ps. 2:6), and it was where God's deeds were to be proclaimed to the world (Ps. 9:11). Isaiah prophesied:

Many peoples shall come and say,
'Come, let us go up to the mountain of the LORD,
　　to the house of the God of Jacob;
that he may teach us his ways
　　and that we may walk in his paths.'
For out of Zion shall go forth instruction,
　　and the word of the LORD from Jerusalem.

(Isa. 2:3)

In the New Testament this becomes the role of the Christian community, sent and embodied in each place. If the local church is to bear witness to the life of the future in the present, then its way of life is meant to show the whole of society God's healthy form of living.

We saw earlier that the state depends on the nation having sufficient shared values of the right sort, but that it does not manufacture those values itself. Like the state, the church does not manufacture the values it follows, but the One who is the source of them grows them in his church. Hence Paul's language of the fruit of the Spirit: the fruit that the Spirit grows. The values needed for public discipleship come through encounter with God in community. 'Religious communities are not communities manufacturing and then maintaining values. Values for them are grounded in an attempt to understand external reality at its most profound level. In short they are grounded in metaphysics.'[2]

Three dimensions of church life: up, in and out[3]

If the local church has such a high calling and such a strategic role in God's purposes for the world, and if it is to be the crucible for discipleship and Christian character, we would expect an ecology in its life which can fulfil the responsibility God has given it. This is best described as life in three directions: up, in, and out.

Up to God: Worship

Up is towards God in worship, prayer and faith. Worship lies at the heart of all Christian civic involvement, because the primary expression of Christian citizenship, 'Jesus is Lord', is an expression of worship, before it is anything else. As Matthew's Gospel reaches its conclusion, Jesus declares, 'All authority in heaven and on earth has been given to me' (Matt. 28:18). He makes this declaration in a context of worship. 'When they saw him, they worshipped him' (this was honest worship: 'but some doubted', 28:17).

Paul wrote to the Philippians, 'We . . . worship in the Spirit of God and boast in Christ Jesus and have no confidence in the flesh' (Phil. 3:3). If Christian citizenship is embodied in involved distinctiveness and subversive engagement, then it has great confidence in God's purposes for his creation through Christ and by the Spirit, but no confidence in an age that is passing away. In this light, joyful worship 'is evidence that we have moved from security in self-esteem to security in being recognised and loved by the triune God'.[4] At the heart of true worship is gratitude, the virtue which is the key to all the others. Gratitude lies at the heart of our worship of God and of our service in society.

This is not a book on worship, so it is important to state clearly that worship is always to God, for God and about God. Worship is integral to shaping a life of discipleship, but disciple-making is not the primary purpose of worship. It is a bonus, due entirely to the ecology of God's grace. If the 'up' to God is not primarily for God, it becomes another form of self-seeking. However, in the ecology of grace there is a direct connection between worship and the quality of our lives. 'If worship of God is at the centre of Christian worship, then the moral life may flow from this worship. The moral life is not the main object of worship, but it should be a fruit of it.'[5]

Worship must be personal, but like the rest of the Christian life, it is essentially corporate. It should never be an individualist's charter. We were baptized into Christ, buried and raised with him. But our new, risen identity is a corporate one. 'For just as the body is one and has many members, and all the members of the body, though many, are one body, so it is with Christ. For in the one Spirit we were all baptized into one body – Jews or Greeks, slaves or free – and we were all made to drink of one Spirit' (1 Cor. 12:12–13). In a parallel passage in his letter to Rome, Paul wrote, 'I appeal to you therefore, brothers and sisters, by the mercies of God, to present your bodies as a living sacrifice, holy and acceptable to God, which is your spiritual worship' (Rom. 12:1). Spiritual worship involves community. It means offering our bodies to God as *one* living sacrifice. In many ways, when the church is scattered, our personal worship is a form of gathered worship 'by extension'. When Jesus taught his disciples to pray alone, and in secret, he told them to pray 'our Father'. The Lord's Prayer is an 'us' prayer, not a 'me' prayer.[6] But in this shared encounter with God, we do not lose our God-given individuality; rather we find our true selves. 'There are similar selves being transformed; yet the faces resist collectivisation. It is a picture of intensified community and intensified individuality together, gathered before the one whose love compels each in joyful responsibility.'[7] Regular corporate worship is a central joyful discipline of Christian discipleship.

The statement in *Citizenship in Britain* that governments do not and cannot create the values upon which both government and citizenship depend, raises an obvious question. Where are they formed, then? Worship provides a major part of the answer, not just for religious communities, but for all people, because all people worship. The same biblical word can be translated as 'worship' or 'serve'. For example, Jesus said, 'No one can serve two masters; for a slave will either hate the one and love the other, or be devoted to the one and despise the other. You cannot serve God and wealth' (Matt. 6:24). What we serve shapes us. Our heart will always be where our treasure is. The Bible is full of warnings about false worship, or idolatry, because it involves a double dishonouring of God. The first dishonouring comes through offering the devotion due to God to something less than God, which is not worthy of worship. The second dishonouring comes when our character starts to be shaped by the object of our worship. Those who worship the Father through his Son and by his Spirit begin to take on the family likeness of heaven. The broken divine image becomes the object of major restoration. False worship further distorts the divine image.

Christian worship is transformative. Paul's appeal for the presentation of our bodies as one living sacrifice continues with an expectation of transformation. 'Do not be conformed to this world, but be transformed by the renewing of your minds, so that you may discern what is the will of God – what is good and acceptable and perfect' (Rom. 12:2). In response to his mercies, we come before God on the basis of what we know of him through Scripture. We pray the Scriptures back to him, trust their promises, sing praises, old and new, based on his word. We confess our sin, in the light of his revelation. Through faith in his atoning death, we receive forgiveness and renew our commitment to him. We receive new light from Scripture and a fresh anointing from his Spirit. We break bread and share wine, as he commanded, in his presence, anticipating his final coming. Through it all we give thanks. Pervading it all is God's presence. 'We worship', said Paul, 'in the Holy Spirit.' And the Holy Spirit brings the presence and foretaste of God's kingdom. So 'worship may be described as an event in which the kingdom of God is "in a manner" actually and freely present – and not merely future'.[8] 'Those who do so usually believe that, in worship, we touch the deepest level of reality. We come into the very presence of the Creator.'[9] How can it not be transformative?

Corporate worship refocuses us on our true identity, renews us in hope and sharpens our sense of calling to serve God in his world. 'Within worship moral values take on a more demanding and insistent shape, than they do outside worship: they change the very way we see the world.'[10]

The worship of the early church was one of the great keys to its growth and to its profound impact on the Roman Empire. But this impact was indirect. Worship was not treated as the church's shop window. It was far too dangerous to give an open invitation to any pagan who wanted to come. In fact, new converts underwent an extensive preparation before they were allowed to meet the majority of the local Christian community and join it in worship.[11] But in authentic worship, believers were transformed. Involved distinctiveness and subversive engagement became possible, because God was shaping them as people who could live that way.

> Worship, to which pagans were denied admission, was all important
> in the spread of the church. It was important not because it was
> attractive, but because its rites and practices made differences in the
> lives and communities of the worshippers. It performed the function
> of re-forming those pagans who joined the church into Christians, into
> distinctive people who lived in a way that was recognisably in the
> tradition of Jesus Christ.[12]

Still today, 'Worship makes strong demands upon us. It requires no less than we should go out into the world to love, serve and care.'[13]

This might sound very theoretical, but fortunately there is evidence of the impact of worship upon behaviour. Professor Robin Gill reports on 'a measurable link between worship and moral action in the community'.[14] 'Empirically it would seem that those undertaking selfless care belong disproportionately to worshipping communities.'[15] A higher proportion of regular worshippers serve, for no personal return, than is the case among those who do not worship. Leslie Francis's studies in young people's attitudes and behaviour provide a similar result. Young people who worship regularly show a greater tendency to serve and care than do those who worship occasionally, who again outperform those who never worship.[16] Even more remarkable was the 'testimony' of the Labour politician Roy Hattersley in the *Guardian* newspaper. In a piece headed 'We atheists have to accept that believers are better human beings', he commented:

> Civilised people [presumably like himself!] do not believe that drug addiction and male prostitution offend against divine ordinance. But those who do are the men and women most willing to change the fetid bandages, replace the sodden sleeping bags and – probably most difficult of all – argue, without a trace of impatience, that the time has come for some serious medical treatment. Good works, John Wesley insisted, are no guarantee of a place in heaven. But they are most likely to be performed by people who believe that heaven exists. The correlation is so clear that it is impossible to doubt that faith and charity go hand in hand.

With far more than grudging respect, he added:

> The only possible conclusion is that faith comes with a packet of moral imperatives that, while they do not condition the attitude of all believers, influence enough of them to make them morally superior to atheists like me. The truth may make us free. But it has not made us as admirable as the average captain in the Salvation Army.[17]

Like Roy Hattersley, I am not claiming that all worshippers end up as active Christian citizens. In fact, the challenge is for worshippers to ensure that their worship of God is linked to the fullest vision God has revealed of his purposes and plans for the earth. But worship can grow values. It is a vital resource for public discipleship.

Personal spiritual disciplines

The central importance of corporate worship does not replace the need for personal spiritual disciplines. Jesus' yoke may be easy and his burden light, but we are still called to take that yoke upon us, and learn from him (Matt. 11:28–30). Earlier in this section, I said that 'How may Jesus be formed in me?' was a better question than 'What would Jesus do?' Dallas Willard makes the same point.

Asking ourselves 'What would Jesus do?' when suddenly in the face
of an important situation simply is not an adequate discipline or
preparation to enable one to live as he lived ... The secret of the easy
yoke, then, is to learn from Christ how to live our total lives, how to
invest all our energies of mind and body as he did. We must learn
how to follow his preparations, the disciplines for life in God's rule
that enabled him to receive his Father's constant and effective support
while doing his will.[18]

Willard makes the obvious but vital point that Jesus is our primary
example if we want to learn how to grow as disciples. His prioritizing
of prayer, his knowledge of Scripture and his capacity to see his
Father at work are all essential disciplines and skills we need
to develop.

In public discipleship, 'what you see is what you get' will not
suffice. Our lives must be lives of integrity, but there needs to be
more to us than people see. The challenge is to be an iceberg for
God. The key question is, how much of you is below the surface?
Personal disciplines are about a secret life before God.

Mostly the Bible condemns secret lives and warns that on the
day of judgment all secrets will be revealed.[19] But Jesus encouraged a different sort of secret life – a life of discipleship that is
secret, known only to God, because it is not seeking any im-
mediate reward.

Beware of practising your piety before others in order to be seen
by them; for then you have no reward from your Father in
heaven.

So whenever you give alms, do not sound a trumpet before you,
as the hypocrites do in the synagogues and in the streets, so that they
may be praised by others. Truly I tell you, they have received their
reward. But when you give alms, do not let your left hand know what
your right hand is doing, so that your alms may be done in secret;
and your Father who sees in secret will reward you.

And whenever you pray, do not be like the hypocrites; for they
love to stand and pray in the synagogues and at the street corners, so
that they may be seen by others. Truly I tell you, they have received
their reward ...

And whenever you fast, do not look dismal, like the hypocrites, for
they disfigure their faces so as to show others that they are fasting.
Truly I tell you, they have received their reward . . .
(Matt 6:1–17)

Jesus speaks of prayer – secret time with God; of giving – secret
generosity; and of fasting – secret self-denial. A hidden life which
serves God in these ways builds in us the character to act selflessly,
regardless of the knowledge or reactions of others.

At the heart of any church which knows it is called to public
discipleship will be intercessory prayer. The call to Christian
citizenship is simultaneously a call to action and a conviction that
action alone will not do. Human life was designed to be a partnership with God. Prayer lies at the heart of that partnership. One of
the most encouraging developments in recent years has been the
emergence of the 24/7 prayer movement. Secret intercession may
well be the key to public change.

This is not a book about personal devotions, and there are
excellent books available on spiritual disciplines.[20] But the cultivation
of character comes in part from a disciplined secret life before God.
This may not be popular in our comfortable, quick-solution society,
but there is no way round it if we are serious about discipleship. Jesus
motivated his first followers by setting the bar high, while being full
of compassion. He does the same today.

In to one another

Western culture has undergone a massive turn inwards. Through a
combination of the Enlightenment and Romanticism, we have
become convinced that the answer to everything lies inside the
individual. In the second section of this book, we saw how that has
contributed to individualism and how our consumer culture operates
in response to our emotional needs. From a biblical point of view, this
journey into the interior is a journey in the wrong direction. It is
through relationships that potential is developed and character grown.

Paul's letters are full of the phrase 'one another'. It appears thirty-
four times.[21] It is clear that he believed mutual relationships to be
the essence of a local church. This is spelled out graphically in
1 Corinthians 12. No Christian can say, 'I have no need of you.'

In Ephesians, growth to maturity depends on 'every part working properly'.

One aspect of this is directly relevant to our theme. The purpose of Christian relationships is to form a way of life worthy of the gospel.

In the New Testament, two major strategies are used against the church: one is persecution and the other is seduction. In times of persecution, the community is vital for support.[22] Seduction, however, is a more subtle form of assault. We saw in 1 Corinthians how powerful some of these temptations could be, just because everyone in that social class played the status game. 'It was not a change of heart that might win a Christian convert back to paganism, but the overwhelming pressure to conform imposed by the institutions of his city and the activities of his neighbour.'[23]

The letter to the Hebrews was written to a group of Jewish Christians who were tempted to return to their previous faith community because of the safety it offered them. Whether under persecution, or in our Western culture which has turned seduction into an art form, the purpose of our relationships within the body of Christ is to establish and maintain a distinctively Christian way of life. 'You do not need a strong community, the church, to support an ethic everyone else already affirms ... Christian community is not primarily about togetherness ... togetherness happens but only as a by-product of the main project of trying to be *faithful to Jesus*.'[24] The letter to the Hebrews addresses this very practically.

> Take care, brothers and sisters, that none of you may have an evil,
> unbelieving heart that turns away from the living God. But exhort
> one another every day, as long as it is called 'today', so that none of
> you may be hardened by the deceitfulness of sin. For we have become
> partners of Christ, if only we hold our first confidence firm to the end.
> (Heb. 3:12–14)

Here is a straightforward recognition that Christians may be called to distinctive public discipleship, and churches may be designed to be the crucibles for Christian character, but there is a real potential to fail. So Christians are expected to hold one another to account for their discipleship. Personal lifestyle questions are to be the daily subject matter within Christian relationships. Faith is applied to life and life decisions shared. Roles of service in the community can be prayed for and supported, and so on.

Seduction works because sin is deceitful. Christians need to guard one another's backs and be in one another's faces. We are also called to a proactive ministry of encouragement. This clearly requires a discipline of regular meeting. 'And let us consider how to provoke one another to love and good deeds, not neglecting to meet together, as is the habit of some, but encouraging one another, and all the more as you see the Day approaching' (Heb. 10:24–25). This is a long way from the average church home group, because it is based on two underlying assumptions. First, that the church is intended to be a community of discipleship, not just a place of worship. Second, that Christians are meant to be accountable to one another. 'The church is marked by community, inter-personal relationships, mutuality and interdependence.'[25]

This form of mutual accountability is like the quality control department for the church's public witness. It is a mutual responsibility to ensure that all local witness is Christ-like. As Jim Wallis said, 'We have nothing to share with the world than what we are sharing with each other. We can effect no change in the ways of the world, unless we ourselves are being converted from those ways.'[26] The church is the crucible for ongoing conversion; for Christ being formed in us.

In the last section, we saw from 1 Corinthians 12 how Paul took the image of the body, which was used in his culture as a way of keeping each person in their 'proper' social place, and revolutionized it. The result was 'a form of solidarity, constructed through reversing the conventional positions of high and low, wise and foolish, honourable and dishonourable, and fostering instead a mutual and egalitarian other-regard'.[27]

This principle has been used at various times throughout church history: in New Testament house churches, in small monastic communities, in Wesley's class and band meetings, in today's global explosion of the cell church concept. The key emphasis must be growth in discipleship through mutual encouragement and mutual accountability.

A key New Testament term is 'to build up'. I used to regard it as a verb used almost entirely about the internal life of the church, particularly in worship. 'Since you are eager for spiritual gifts, strive to excel in them for building up the church ... What should be done then, my friends? When you come together ... Let all things be done for building up' (1 Cor. 14:12, 26). But that is not the case. As we shall see, it is used just as often for the impact of believers on those outside the church.

Here is a community in which 'edification', the building up of others, is the purpose of its internal relationships, but also the purpose of its relationships with non-believers. It is called the local church.

Out to the world

Paul's expression 'building up' provides the bridge between the 'in' to one another and the 'out' to the world, indicating that Paul could not imagine one without the other. 'Each of us must please our neighbour for the good purpose of building up the neighbour' (Rom. 15:2). ' "All things are lawful," but not all things are beneficial. "All things are lawful," but not all things build up' (1 Cor. 10:23). 'Let no evil talk come out of your mouths, but only what is useful for building up, as there is need, so that your words may give grace to those who hear' (Eph. 4:29).

Every Christian is to be a benefactor. We saw in the first section the clear expectation that the early Christians were to be identified by their good deeds, by the way in which even the socially powerless acted as benefactors and pursued other people's advantage, and by their practical love of their neighbours as themselves. This material appears from the earliest follow-up letters, once a church had been planted and the apostle (in this case Paul) had moved on. It is mentioned in passing rather than developed as a new theme, and must have been part of the initial instruction in the faith given to new believers. This reminds me of an aside made by the Rev. John Wimber of the Anaheim Vineyard. John had been describing the hundreds of members of his church who worked in the church's projects among the poor each Saturday. Many of them were newish converts, with little concept of what church was meant to be. 'They don't know any better,' he said, 'and you don't tell them any different.' In Paul's churches, to be a blessing to your neighbour was normal Christianity. They didn't know any better either.

This is, of course, entirely coherent with the teaching of Jesus, who refused to allow any split between the command to love God and the command to love neighbour.[28] God's covenant people were not given a choice between the first four commandments, which summarized their duty towards God, and the remaining six, which expressed their responsibilities to one another. The love of God could not be separated from the love of neighbour.

Jesus healed the sick, gave hope to the poor and even fed the hungry, without asking anyone to make a commitment first or to sign a doctrinal basis before he would pray for them. He told his disciples to keep their prayer, fasting and giving secret, but to 'let your light shine before others, so that they may see your good works and give glory to your Father in heaven' (Matt. 5:16).

Late in his ministry, Paul would make the theology for this quite clear. It is all a response to grace, and all within God's plan for a new creation. 'For by grace you have been saved through faith, and this is not your own doing; it is the gift of God – not the result of works, so that no one may boast. For we are what he has made us, created in Christ Jesus for good works, which God prepared beforehand to be our way of life' (Eph. 2:8–10). The doing of good to our neighbour is our way of life. It could not be put simpler than that.

In more ways than one, Christian public discipleship is walking in the footsteps of Jesus. So the practice of each Christian, envisioned by worship, undergirded by personal prayer and study, and accountable to a supporting small group, should include the discipline of service. Particular attention should be given to those to whom Jesus gave priority in his ministry and teaching: the poor or powerless, the sick, the prisoner, the homeless, the widow or orphan, the alien or stranger, and so on.

If such disciples also have or are given positions of influence in society, they will exercise their power with an empathy for the last and the least. They will have learned, by habit, to share Christ's heart for the needy. Local churches should have programmes in which their members can join. Better still, their members will identify opportunities for service in which their brothers and sisters can join. Above all, this is to be a daily way of life.

Public discipleship cannot be learned in a classroom, or even by reading this book. It has to be learned in practice, by identifying and taking advantage of the opportunities Christ has provided and for which we were recreated. 'How does one acquire the Christian virtues? The short answer is, by practising the Christian life.'[29]

Is this mere idealism?

Is this mere idealism? It had better not be, because I see no alternative in Scripture to the local church as the crucible for public discipleship. This may raise questions about the purpose and quality of many a local fellowship. However, if the Spirit of God is present among the people of God, then each local church has the potential to live this way. I would like to conclude this section with some positive examples.

Columbus Ohio Vineyard has a ministry called Fruit of the Vine. It is a ministry to people in need. 'Some people say it's about social justice, racial reconciliation, ending hunger and seeing every person treated with the dignity they deserve. We believe that if we follow Jesus in what he is doing we will see all of those things addressed and even more.'[30] They have held events to provide free legal, medical and other services to single parents. This is a biblically orthodox church which does not major on sexual sin, but which believes that homosexual practice is morally wrong. But it also runs the largest support programme for people with HIV / AIDS (many of them gay) in their city. There are no strings. It is simply a ministry of service.

The Eden projects in Greater Manchester began in 1997 and are now in nine deprived estates. Young adults live as a transforming presence and Christian witness in these communities.[31] They are organized by the Message Trust, which is now one of the sponsors of the Greater Manchester annual crime reduction awards.[32] The Salford-based Life Centre opened its doors in 2000, after research in the area demonstrated a need for young people to have a meeting place in the community, where positive programmes could be birthed. All of this work is closely linked to the Manchester City-Wide Prayer Movement.

The day before I gave the lecture upon which this section of the book is based, the *Guardian* newspaper published an article about Eden Openshaw, five years into its ministry.[33] The article says that

Eden is now 'a fundamental part of the local support system'. Andy Hawthorne, the leader of the Message Trust, sums up the vision in this way: 'The gospel changes people's hearts and makes them better citizens. But we have been hiding the light of the gospel message under bushels in church buildings. Our work is incarnational – that's the way The Boss did it.' One community leader is quoted as saying, 'They are normal people who have bought homes and made friends here. What they do works. They're the best thing since sliced bread.'

The Sojourners Community is based in downtown Washington DC.

> Sojourners ministries grew out of the Sojourners Community, located in Southern Columbia Heights, an inner-city neighborhood in Washington, D.C. The community began at Trinity Evangelical Divinity School in Deerfield, Illinois, in the early 1970s when a handful of students began meeting to discuss the relationship between their faith and political issues, particularly the Vietnam War. In 1971, the group decided to create a publication that would express their convictions and test whether other people of faith had similar beliefs. Over the years, however, Sojourners went through a variety of transitions. Slowly, the household communities gave way to an intentional community (with a common rule of life). Today, the community context has shifted away from an intentional model; rather we are a committed group of Christians who work together to live a gospel life that integrates spiritual renewal and social justice.[34]

It is this community which provides Jim Wallis with the base for his ministry into US public life.

In the evangelical history of the UK, Holy Trinity Church, Clapham has a special place. Holy Trinity was the London base of the Saints, sometimes known as the Clapham Sect. It has been called 'perhaps the most notable congregation in England'.[35] Under the leadership of the Rev. John Venn, they were devoted to the church, fervent in prayer (following a rule of life which set aside three separate hours a day for intercessory prayer), generous with time and money, inspired by studying the Bible, and joyful. Two months before his death, John Venn wrote to his children, 'You can all bear witness that I have never represented religion as a gloomy thing,

I have never said you must do this or you will go to hell, but I have set
it before you as a scene of joy and happiness unspeakable.' The Saints
were well-to-do and influential people who used their influence to
benefit society as a whole. They were central to the campaign against
slavery, bringing to the campaign 'a dedication that forced them to
act'.[36] It is doubtful whether a single small congregation has in the
history of Christendom exercised such a far-flung influence. They

- fostered evangelical Christianity;
- encouraged the Church Missionary Society and the British and
  Foreign Bible Society;
- encouraged the good administration of India and Sierra Leone;
- encouraged education and backed Robert Raikes's Sunday
  School movement;
- supported the Factory Act;
- made provision for the poor;
- attacked blood sports, duelling and gambling;
- set higher standards of morality in public life;
- set higher standards of active concern in politics;
- and, of course, abolished the slave trade.

They were people of their time, but so are we. Why can't it happen
again today? It is called public discipleship.

Notes

1 Robin Gill, *Moral Communities*, Exeter: Exeter University Press, 1992,
   p. 13.
2 Ibid., p. 55f.
3 This pattern is found in a number of Christian sources. I met it first
   in the strategy document of a youth congregation in Cheltenham.
   A primary source is the Lifeshapes material, developed by the Rev.
   Mike Breen in Sheffield, now published as *A Passionate Life* and
   A Passionate Church, by Mike Breen and Walt Kallestad, Eastbourne:
   Kingsway, 2005.
4 David Ford, *Salvation*, Cambridge: Cambridge University Press, 1999,
   p. 100.
5 Robin Gill, *Church Growth*, London: SPCK, 1994, p. 19.

6   See Matt. 6:5–13.

7   Ford, *Salvation*, p. 103.

8   Alan Torrance, *Persons in Communion*, Edinburgh: T. & T. Clark, 1996, p. 312.

9   Robin Gill, *A Vision for Growth*, London: SPCK, 1994, p. 19.

10 Gill, *Moral Communities*, p. 81.

11 In New Testament Corinth, non-Christians could attend Christian worship (1 Cor. 14:24), but in the post-apostolic period, once Christianity was regarded as an illegal religion, rather than a Jewish sect, the church had to protect its worship for its own safety.

12 Alan Kreider, *Worship and Evangelism in Pre-Christendom*, Cambridge: Grove Joint Liturgical Studies 32, 1995, p. 10.

13 Gill, *Moral Communities*, p. 23.

14 Ibid., p. 20.

15 Ibid., p. 51.

16 For a detailed study of all this, including Francis's work, see Robin Gill, *Church Going and Christian Ethics*, Cambridge: Cambridge University Press, 1999.

17 Roy Hattersley, *Guardian*, 12 September 2005.

18 Dallas Willard, *The Spirit of the Disciplines*, San Francisco: Harper & Row, 1988, p. 9 (I strongly recommend Willard's books).

19 E.g. Matt. 10:26; Rom. 2:16.

20 I recommend Richard Foster, *The Celebration of Discipline*, London: Hodder & Stoughton, 1980; and Dallas Willard, *The Spirit of the Disciplines*, and *The Divine Conspiracy*, London: Fount, 1998.

21 Rom. 12:10, 16; 13:8; 14:13; 15:5, 7, 14; 16:16; 1 Cor. 6:7; 7:5; 11:33; 12:25; 16:20; 2 Cor. 10:12; 2 Cor. 13:11, 12; Gal. 5:13, 15, 26; 6:2; Eph. 4:2, 25, 32; 5:21; Col. 3:9, 13, 16; 1 Thess. 3:12; 4:9, 18; 5:11, 15; 2 Thess. 1:3; Titus 3:3.

22 E.g. Heb. 10:30–36; 13:3; 1 Pet. 4:12–14.

23 S. Mitchell, in Bruce Winter, *After Paul Left Corinth*, Grand Rapids: Eerdmans, 2001, p. 95.

24 Stanley Hauerwas and William Willimon, *Resident Aliens*, Abingdon: Nashville, 1989, pp. 73, 78.

25 Howard Snyder, *The Community of the King*, Downers Grove: IVP, 1977, p. 67.

26 Jim Wallis, *The Call to Conversion*, New York: Harper & Row, 1981, p. 125.

27 David Horrell, *Solidarity and Difference*, Edinburgh: T. & T. Clark, 2005, p. 124.

28 See Mark 12:28–31, where Jesus is asked about the first commandment of all. He replies with two.

29 See Heb. 3:12–14.

30 www.vineyardcolumbus.org/ministries/fotv.

31 See Matt Wilson, *Eden: Called to the Streets*, Eastbourne: Survivor, 2005.

32 www.message.org.uk.

33 http://society.guardian.co.uk/socialexclusion/story/0,11499,1606107,00.html.

34 www.sojo.net/index.cfm?action=about_us.home.

35 Nigel Scotland, *Evangelical Anglicans*, Carlisle: Paternoster, 2004, pp. 27–30.

36 David Bebbington, *Evangelicalism in Modern Britain*, London: Unwin Hyman, 1989, p. 71.

Section Four

The Transformation of Community

The examples given at the close of the last chapter show that Christians can expect to have a positive influence on society. We can contribute to the public or civic sphere, and to the common good, in the light of the gospel. But it is all too easy to give good examples and success stories. What is needed is a clear theological vision for our involvement. In this section, I will spell out the shape of that vision.

Called to be a forward-looking church

Much Christian involvement in society is negative. Too often we are best known for what we are against, rather than what we are for. There is a valid and honourable role in being the salt of the earth, preserving our society from evil and moral decay, but salt also adds flavour. The metaphor of salt also implies that there is good in society that is worth preserving. The Creator's image in human society has not been erased, just marred.

As we saw from the church in Corinth, common ground can be found, and should be found when it can. The gospel has had an impact on our society in many previous generations and we should not be surprised to find the evidence. A great deal of the societal fruit that today's culture values was grown on the Christian tree.

The church *is* called to a prophetic ministry, but there is more to the prophetic than denunciation. God has given us a more positive role: like our Lord, we are the light of the world. Light shows the way (like the pillar of fire by day in the exodus story). The people of God are intended to have a pathfinding role for the future of society.

The church is not for church. It does not exist for itself. It exists to embody God's purposes for his creation. That may involve actions and statements which can be seen as negative, but they will always have a positive purpose. The most pathological condition a church can reach is when all its energies are taken up with its own maintenance and survival. 'Churches are occupied with an obsessive struggle just to repeat the past, to survive or to offer shelter from the storm ... Nevertheless, God's intention for the fulfilment of the whole creation is always the Church's horizon.'[1] This is a pathological condition, because it is precisely the opposite of our calling. 'The Church does more than merely point to a reality beyond itself. By virtue of its participation in the life of God, it is not only a sign and an instrument, but also a genuine foretaste of God's Kingdom, called to show forth visibly, in the midst of history, God's final purposes for humankind.'[2]

That is very scary. It is far from most Christians' understanding of the church. It is a long way from the reality of many churches I know. But that is the most biblical statement about the purpose of the church that I have found. 'The church is called to show forth visibly, in the midst of history, God's final purposes for humankind.'

It is time to turn back and justify an assumption made in the first section. Christian discipleship involves living in the present in the light and hope of the future, which Christ has secured.

New heavens and a new earth

Christian life is life which finds its orientation from the future. 'To be a Christian, a person of faith, is precisely to live as a person for whom God's future shapes the present.'[3]

At first this may seem a strange claim. Our faith is rooted in what God has done in Christ in the past. We inherit the gospel from the past, and are called to pass it on unaltered. To quote 1 Corinthians again, 'I handed on to you as of first importance what I in turn had received: that Christ died for our sins in accordance with the scriptures, and that he was buried, and that he was raised on the third day in accordance with the scriptures' (1 Cor. 15:3–4). We are called to treasure and pass on the inheritance we have received from the past. The core act of Christian worship is the Holy Communion, which is based on remembering what Christ has done.

> For I received from the Lord what I also handed on to you, that the Lord Jesus on the night when he was betrayed took a loaf of bread, and when he had given thanks, he broke it and said, 'This is my body that is for you. Do this in remembrance of me.' In the same way he took the cup also, after supper, saying, 'This cup is the new covenant in my blood. Do this, as often as you drink it, in remembrance of me.' (1 Cor. 11:23–25)

But the following verse gives the clue. 'For as often as you eat this bread and drink the cup, you proclaim the Lord's death until he comes' (v. 26). The Christian faith is forward-looking precisely because what Christ has done in the past has secured the future. We look back, in faith and gratitude, so that we might look forward. What Christ has done in the past has secured our future, which releases us to work for the future of others, because we have no need for long-term anxiety about ourselves. Paul's great statement about passing on what he had received is at the beginning of a majestic chapter about a future secured by the resurrection, to which we will return soon.

The biblical promise

The foundational biblical promise, upon which the whole practice of Christian citizenship depends, is the promise of new heavens and a new earth. This may surprise those who believe that salvation is about 'going to heaven when we die'. But the Bible moves from creation to new creation. Christian citizenship is based on the conviction that the earth has a future in God's purposes.

New creation is an Old Testament promise, further developed in the New Testament. I will quote the key passage in full.

> For I am about to create new heavens
>   and a new earth;
> the former things shall not be remembered
>   or come to mind.
> But be glad and rejoice forever
>   in what I am creating;
> for I am about to create Jerusalem as a joy,
>   and its people as a delight.
> I will rejoice in Jerusalem,
>   and delight in my people;
> no more shall the sound of weeping be heard in it,
>   or the cry of distress.
> No more shall there be in it
>   an infant that lives but a few days,
>   or an old person who does not live out a lifetime;
> for one who dies at a hundred years will be considered a youth,
>   and one who falls short of a hundred will be considered accursed.
> They shall build houses and inhabit them;
>   they shall plant vineyards and eat their fruit.
> They shall not build and another inhabit;
>   they shall not plant and another eat;
> for like the days of a tree shall the days of my people be,
>   and my chosen shall long enjoy the work of their hands.
> They shall not labour in vain,
>   or bear children for calamity;
> for they shall be offspring blessed by the LORD –
>   and their descendants as well.
> Before they call I will answer,
>   while they are yet speaking I will hear.
> The wolf and the lamb shall feed together,
>   the lion shall eat straw like the ox;
>   but the serpent – its food shall be dust!
> They shall not hurt or destroy
>   on all my holy mountain, says the LORD.
> (Isa. 65:17–25)

There is no hint of the end of the world here, nor even of the end of history. Instead we are given a vision of the climax of history, which is not the same thing. Although the passage promises 'new heavens', it is primarily a picture of a new earth. It is a very physical vision, of a world free from suffering and injustice, a world in which there is no infant mortality or premature death. People enjoy the fruit of their labour and no thief, corrupt boss or invader takes it from them. People enjoy open communion with God, who answers their prayers even as they are being spoken. Up to this point, Isaiah seems to be speaking of the creation as we know it, with the effects of human sin removed. But verse 25 hints of something more: 'The wolf and the lamb shall feed together, the lion shall eat straw like the ox; but the serpent – its food shall be dust! They shall not hurt or destroy on all my holy mountain, says the LORD.' Here is a hint of creation being more than it was before, of a different quality, with every consequence of evil (note the reference to the serpent) gone.

Just as Isaiah has the Genesis stories of creation and fall in mind, so in the New Testament his language is taken up and taken further. The Old Testament has a less clear grasp of life after death than the New. As we shall see, it is the resurrection of Jesus which is the great guarantee of our eternal future, and of the renewal of creation. The resurrection will enlarge Isaiah's vision, but it will not make it less. The physical world matters, not only because God made it 'good', but because God will make it new. When God created humankind out of the same stuff as the rest of creation, he declared it to be 'very good'. Human birth and death, life and work, food and shelter matter to God. How we live with one another matters to God. If God will one day make the earth 'new', we need to care for it and for one another now. New Testament mission will never be less practical than this.

This Old Testament passage has been used as a Christian basis for local mission. Called 'The Isaiah Vision',[4] it identifies four key issues with which local churches can engage: 'that children do not die, that old people live in dignity, that those who build houses live in them, that those who plant vineyards eat the fruit'. Locally adapted, it provides a good example of a strategy for public discipleship and Christian citizenship.

The theme of the new heaven(s) and new earth is taken up, directly and indirectly, in the New Testament. But the question arises: how new is new? Does new mean that the old one has been thrown away because it is (literally) beyond redemption? A superficial reading of the most vivid passage would appear to say so.

> But the day of the Lord will come like a thief, and then the heavens will pass away with a loud noise, and the elements will be dissolved with fire, and the earth and everything that is done on it will be disclosed.
>
> Since all these things are to be dissolved in this way, what sort of persons ought you to be in leading lives of holiness and godliness, waiting for and hastening the coming of the day of God, because of which the heavens will be set ablaze and dissolved, and the elements will melt with fire? But, in accordance with his promise, we wait for new heavens and a new earth, where righteousness is at home.
> (2 Pet. 3:10–13)

If the elements will 'melt' and the heavens be 'dissolved' and we wait for 'new' heavens and earth, it does sound as though the old one will be incinerated to make way for the new one. The ethical significance of this would be drastic. In our homes we do not take a lot of care of things we are about to throw in the fire or put on the tip! Why care for the environment, for example, if it is all going to be burned up anyway? There would be no point in Christian citizenship if discipleship meant keeping our head down in public and waiting for the fire, in the assurance that we had been saved from it. Years ago, at the Greenbelt Festival, a well-meaning Christian singer stood on the concert stage and said he would welcome a nuclear attack because it would mean he and his family would go immediately to be with Jesus! I and the other organizers groaned, because unbeknown to the singer, that year's festival was running a series of seminars on a Christian response to the threat of nuclear war and the policy of deterrence. The difference between Christian citizenship and head-in-the-sand pietism could not have been clearer. Our vision of the future that God has promised shapes the way we live on earth in the present.

But we need to take a more careful look at 2 Peter. Even if 'new' does mean 'replaced', Peter is teaching that the future world is not heaven when we die, with the earth as a fading memory, but new heavens and a new earth. The earth is part of God's eternal future for humankind. 'New' here does not mean 'replaced', but 'renewed', made new, exactly as Isaiah promised. There are two Greek words for 'new'. One means new as in 'throw it away and get a new one'. The other means new as in 'renewed, restored to being all that it was made to be and had the potential to be'. It is this word that the New Testament *always* uses when it speaks of the new earth. 'New creation is . . . an act which preserves the identity of the first creation while creatively transforming it.'[5]

What, then, of all the imagery about fire, melting, dissolving and so on? This is standard biblical language for the fire of purification and of final judgment. Our faith is tested by the fire of various trials so that it may be shown to be genuine when Christ is revealed.[6] The work we have done is tested through fire, so the things which have been built on Christ (gold, silver and precious stones) may survive the fire in which the wood, hay and stubble are burned up.[7] True faith survives the fire. The work which has Christ as its foundation survives the fire. We who are in Christ survive the fire, although we may not keep with us everything we had imagined! Human history is put through the fire, and only what is good survives. In the same way, a renewed earth survives the fire, and emerges in its original purity. Fire does speak of destruction, but only the destruction of evil.

This pattern of radical judgment and yet continuity is identical to God's dealing with us. To become a Christian is both a death (buried with Christ) and a resurrection (raised with Christ). This is put very clearly in Galatians: 'I have been crucified with Christ; and it is no longer I who live, but it is Christ who lives in me. And the life I now live in the flesh I live by faith in the Son of God, who loved me and gave himself for me' (Gal. 2:19–20). In this passage there is a death, an ending, and yet the same (but 'new') 'I' now lives, with Christ indwelling. God's promise about the earth is identical. He will renew it, and the renewed earth will have Christ at its centre.

This takes us to Revelation 21. The Bible concludes with a magnificent description of the climax of all God's re-creative work.

Then I saw a new heaven and a new earth; for the first heaven and the first earth had passed away, and the sea was no more. And I saw

the holy city, the new Jerusalem, coming down out of heaven from
God, prepared as a bride adorned for her husband. And I heard a loud
voice from the throne saying,

'See, the home of God is among mortals.

He will dwell with them;

they will be his peoples,

and God himself will be with them;

he will wipe every tear from their eyes.

Death will be no more;

mourning and crying and pain will be no more,

for the first things have passed away.'

And the one who was seated on the throne said, 'See, I am making all
things new.'

(Rev. 21:1–5)

At the climax of creation, as at the beginning of creation, God will do
what only God can do. The making new of heaven and earth will
be 'a fresh creative act of the transcendent God, who would thus
make of his creation what it had no immanent capacity to be'.[8] The
implication of all this for Christian citizenship is clear. The renewal of
the earth is a divine activity, not a human one. We cannot build
Jerusalem in England's green and pleasant land, nor anywhere else!
But in the name of God's Son and in the power of God's Spirit, we
can be fellow workers with God in all that he is doing ahead of and
towards that great day.

In Revelation, Isaiah 65 is both fulfilled and surpassed, for death is
no more. Jerusalem is new. In Isaiah's prophecy, Zion represented
the people of God. In Revelation, the holy city represents the New
Testament people of God, the church, described also as the bride of
Christ. The central reality of the new heaven and earth is the
presence of God: 'The home of God is among mortals. He will dwell
with them; they will be his peoples, and God himself will be with
them.' In this scenario, we do not leave the earth to go to heaven,
but God comes to make his home among us. 'I saw no temple in the
city, for its temple is the Lord God the Almighty and the Lamb. And
the city has no need of sun or moon to shine on it, for the glory of
God is its light, and its lamp is the Lamb' (Rev. 21:22–23). Human
history survives to be part of the renewed reality.

The nations will walk by its light, and the kings of the earth will bring their glory into it. Its gates will never be shut by day – and there will be no night there. People will bring into it the glory and the honour of the nations. But nothing unclean will enter it, nor anyone who practises abomination or falsehood, but only those who are written in the Lamb's book of life.
(Rev. 21:24–27)

The purifying fire of God's judgment purges human history. Only those listed in the Lamb's book of life, whose sins have been taken away by his sacrificial death, can survive that profound cleansing. But from the moment they know that their names are written there by grace, they are called to become a part of God's great work, and carriers of God's great invitation. 'The entire universe is summoned by the Spirit to a new future ... a destiny centred on the one who says "Behold I make all things new".'[9]

Other New Testament passages and phrases carry the same message.

'All things'

The 'all things' of Revelation 21:5 is taken up by Paul as well. In Ephesians he says that God has a plan for the fullness of time. He has now set forth that plan in Christ. God's purpose is 'to gather up all things in him, things in heaven and things on earth' (Eph. 1:10). In Colossians this plan is directly linked to the cross. 'Through him God was pleased to reconcile to himself all things, whether on earth or in heaven, by making peace through the blood of his cross' (Col. 1:20).

'Sabbath rest'

The letter to the Hebrews promises a new creation by speaking about the future Sabbath. 'So then, a sabbath rest still remains for the people of God; for those who enter God's rest also cease from their labours as God did from his' (Heb. 4:9–10). 'Hebrews understands this divine Sabbath rest as the rest that God will finally enjoy in the new creation.'[10] Just as God rested on the seventh day of the original creation, so there will be an eternal Sabbath at the completion of the new creation. And God's people will share that rest with him, in his new creation.

Hebrews also uses the language of fire which purifies, saying that this consuming fire reflects the very character of God himself. Hebrews contrasts the giving of the old covenant at Sinai with the giving of the new:

> But now he has promised, 'Yet once more I will shake not only the earth but also the heaven.' This phrase, 'Yet once more,' indicates the removal of what is shaken – that is, created things – so that what cannot be shaken may remain. Therefore, since we are receiving a kingdom that cannot be shaken, let us give thanks, by which we offer to God an acceptable worship with reverence and awe; for indeed our God is a consuming fire. (Heb. 12:26–29)

Earth and heaven will be shaken. Only those things which can endure the consuming fire will remain. But then there will be Sabbath, as the new creation is complete.

The kingdom of God

Above all, Jesus' central theme of the kingdom of God carried the same message of hope for the whole creation. Tom Wright sums up much contemporary scholarship when he says that, in common with his peers,

> [Jesus] believed that the creator God had purposed from the beginning to deal with the problems within his creation *through Israel*. Israel was not just meant to be an 'example' of a nation under God; Israel was to be the means through which the world would be saved. Second, Jesus believed, as did many but not all of his contemporaries, that this vocation would be accomplished through Israel's history reaching a great moment of climax, in which Israel herself would be saved from her enemies, and through which the creator God, the covenant God, would at last bring his love and justice, his mercy and truth, to bear upon the whole world, bringing renewal and healing to all creation.[11]

Note the emphasis on 'the whole world' and 'all creation'. All of this lay behind Jesus' use of the term 'the kingdom of God'. 'The kingdom of God has nothing to do with the world coming to an end.'[12]

The basic theological meaning of the term was 'the new age which replaces the old'. First-century Judaism distinguished between 'this age and the age to come' (a distinction frequently echoed in the New Testament[13]). Following Isaiah and other Old Testament prophecies, the new age would involve the renewal of the whole creation. However, 'Jesus not only made the term the central theme of his proclamation, but, in addition, filled it with a new content which is without analogy'.[14] The unprecedented aspect of Jesus' understanding of the kingdom was that the future rule of God was in some sense present now, and it was present in and through his ministry. With his peers, Jesus still saw human history as divided between two ages, but according to his teaching, the critical dividing point was not the final judgment, but his own proclamation and ministry. Jesus puzzled his contemporaries because his ministry was too great to ignore, but it did not fulfil all their expectations of what should happen when the Messiah came. Even Jesus' cousin and forerunner, John the Baptist, was unsure. While in prison, he sent messengers to question Jesus.

> When the men had come to him, they said, 'John the Baptist has sent us to you to ask, "Are you the one who is to come, or are we to wait for another?" ' Jesus had just then cured many people of diseases, plagues, and evil spirits, and had given sight to many who were blind. And he answered them, 'Go and tell John what you have seen and heard: the blind receive their sight, the lame walk, the lepers are cleansed, the deaf hear, the dead are raised, the poor have good news brought to them. And blessed is anyone who takes no offence at me.' (Luke 7:20–23)

In the new heaven and earth there would be no blindness, lameness, deafness or death. There would be no poverty. The Son of God would be at the heart and centre of the new creation. But this was no longer completely future. In and through Jesus, it was starting now.

This was what Jesus meant when he proclaimed, 'The time is fulfilled, and the kingdom of God has come near' (Mark 1:15). And then, almost immediately, 'Follow me' (v. 17). One scholar has translated his words as 'The revolution is here!'[15] Instead of the new age replacing the old, it had invaded it without totally displacing it. 'The word *revolution* seems calculated to shock and makes the apolitical Christian hearer uneasy. But is that not exactly what Jesus' kingship of God language was bound to do? Kingship no less than revolution was a political term; and to establish a kingship which is not as yet effective *is* to bring about a revolution.'[16]

God's future kingdom is present, in part, now. It is 'the presence of the future'.[17] 'Christ has cleft the future in two, and part of it is already present.'[18] From the time of Jesus' public ministry until the judgment, the ages are in overlap. The kingdom has been inaugurated, but still awaits its consummation and thus has to be understood as both 'already' and 'not yet'.

It is important to grasp the scope of this. God's kingdom is his reign over *all* things, which includes, but cannot be limited to, his inner reign in the hearts of those who believe. 'Neither in Judaism nor elsewhere in the New Testament do we find that the reign of God is something indwelling in men, to be found, say, in the heart; such a spiritualistic understanding is ruled out both for Jesus and for the early Christian tradition.'[19] Consequently, as we saw in his encounter with John the Baptist's messengers, in the public ministry of Jesus, sinners were forgiven, the sick were healed, the demonized were set free, the dead were raised, the hungry were fed, authority was exercised over nature and leaders in public life were challenged. This was all the kingdom of God, because the kingdom of God is God acting as king, God restoring his reign in his fallen world, through his Son Jesus Christ, who taught us all to pray 'Your kingdom come', meaning 'Your will be done on earth as it is in heaven'.

The kingdom is present, as well as future, because the king has come. The kingdom of God is Jesus-shaped!

Perhaps the clearest statement about the future of creation is found in Romans 8.

> For the creation waits with eager longing for the revealing of the children of God; for the creation was subjected to futility, not of its own will but by the will of the one who subjected it, in hope that

the creation itself will be set free from its bondage to decay and will obtain the freedom of the glory of the children of God. We know that the whole creation has been groaning in labour pains until now; and not only the creation, but we ourselves, who have the first fruits of the Spirit, groan inwardly while we wait for adoption, the redemption of our bodies. For in hope we were saved. Now hope that is seen is not hope. For who hopes for what is seen? But if we hope for what we do not see, we wait for it with patience.
(Rom. 8:19–25)

Paul says that the present creation is pregnant with the new creation. The old creation, in which we still live, is 'subject to futility' and in 'bondage to decay'. We might say it has a shelf life, and has no power in itself to extend that shelf life. Like all things within it, one day it will die. But this groaning with futility has been turned into the groaning of labour pains. Because of Christ, a new world is being born. The pain continues. The world is still subject to death. Death is very real. But now there is hope, while the world waits for the new delivery.

When is the due date for the new creation? Amazingly, Paul says, it is the day when the children of God are revealed for who they truly are (the new human race, for the new heavens and earth). Then, when Christ appears, and only then, the creation itself will be set free from its bondage to decay and will obtain the freedom of the glory of the children of God. In other words, the future of creation is directly connected to the future of God's people, the church. Or, to put it another way, the world has no future apart from the church; the church has no future apart from a redeemed world.

I will sum this up with some words from Tom Wright.

God, after all, is the creator; he has no interest in leaving earth to rot and making do for all eternity with only one half of the original creation. God intends to flood the whole cosmos, heaven and earth together, with his presence and grace, and when that happens the new world that results, in which Jesus himself will be the central figure, is to be the inheritance for which Jesus' people are longing.[20]

The earth has a future, and that future has begun.

An ending before a beginning

The world has a future. Creation will be made new, when Christ appears, because of what he has already done.

Incarnation and ascension

Genesis tells us that God regarded the creation of human beings as 'very good' (Gen. 1:31). Colossians tells us that 'all things in heaven and earth' were created in, through and for Christ (Col. 1:16). But John tells us that God's Son, the Word, 'became flesh'. What greater proof can there be that God loves flesh-and-blood human beings, and the planet of which they are the stewards, than that he became one himself? 'In Christ God becomes a part of creation, God is embodied.'[21] Despite our fallen state, God identified with us physically and permanently.

After his death, Christ was raised from the dead in the same flesh and blood, although that flesh and blood were transformed, in the same way as one day the whole earth will be. Nor did he lay aside his humanity when he ascended. The doctrine of the ascension is not a theatrical device to get Jesus off stage. (Exit Jesus, stage above!) The Christ raised and seated at God's right hand is still fully divine and fully human. He did not slip out of his humanity between being taken from our sight on earth and arriving in heaven. Colossians tells us about Christ's incarnation, saying, 'in him all the fullness of God was pleased to dwell' (past tense, Col. 1:19). But the next chapter describes his present condition: 'in him the whole fullness of deity dwells bodily' (present tense, Col. 2:9). In his humanity, he is at the Father's right hand, as our great high priest.[22] 'Jesus has gone in the flesh to the Father.'[23] Wouldn't it be bizarre if the Son of God were to live for eternity in his transformed flesh and blood, while the earth and the rest of the physical universe ceased to exist? David Runcorn put this beautifully when he wrote, 'God wills that we cannot know heaven without also knowing earth.'[24]

We need to learn the full implication of our Lord's incarnation, saving death, resurrection and ascension. Christianity is not a world-escaping faith. It is a world-transforming faith.

> If the incarnation shows us anything, it is that God comes to us and is known by us in and through the created order. This makes our

embodied obedience – our face to face encounters with others, the practice of our work, and our stewardship of the goods of creation – either vehicles of praise or expressions of our indifference to God.[25]

The cross

Up to this point, I have said little about the cross, having jumped from the incarnation to the resurrection. But I did say that the reconciliation of 'all things' was achieved through the cross.[26] One key to understanding this is that the human race are the stewards of the earth. We were given that responsibility at creation.[27] Through our sin we have reneged on that responsibility, treating the world as though it belonged to us and we could do anything with it. Our record has been appalling and we deserve judgment. God has carried out his judgment upon us in Jesus Christ, who died in our place and as our representative. As a consequence, a new, reconciled human race can take up its responsibilities again. 'God's purpose in the death of Christ ... was the removal by death of the sinful humanity that had broken the covenant, and its replacement by a new humanity that would keep and fulfil the covenant.'[28] The cross is the only way to personal salvation, but it has cosmic effect. We should never think of it as merely a transaction about personal salvation; it restores us to our original calling. How bizarre if there was no 'new earth' as part of the inheritance of salvation! 'The cross says that despite its manifest enmity toward God humanity belongs to God; God will not be God without humanity (Rom. 5:10). The cross is the giving up of God's self in order not to give up on humanity.'[29] But if God will not be God without humanity, humanity cannot be humanity without the earth. The cross brings the old human race to an end and the resurrection commences the new creation and the new human race.

Notes

1 Robin Greenwood, *Transforming Church*, London: SPCK, 2002, pp. 11, 13.

2 House of Bishops Report, *Eucharistic Presidency*, London: Church House Publishing, 1997, p. 16.

3 Richard Bauckham and Trevor Hart, *Hope Against Hope*, London: Darton, Longman and Todd, 1999, p. 83.

4 Raymond Fung, *The Isaiah Vision*, Geneva: WCC, 1992.

5 Bauckham and Hart, *Hope Against Hope*, p. 128.

6 See 1 Pet. 1:3–7.

7 See 1 Cor. 3:11–15.

8 Bauckham and Hart, *Hope Against Hope*, p. 38.

9 Jeremy Begbie, *Voicing Creation's Praise*, Edinburgh: T. & T. Clark, 1991, p. 175.

10 Bauckham and Hart, *Hope Against Hope*, p. 155.

11 N. T. Wright, *The Challenge of Jesus*, London: SPCK, 2000, p. 19.

12 Ibid.

13 In Matthew, Mark, Luke, Ephesians and Hebrews.

14 Joachim Jeremias, *New Testament Theology – The Proclamation of Jesus*, London: SCM, 1971, vol. 1, p. 35.

15 David Wenham, *The Parables of Jesus*, London: Hodder & Stoughton, 1989, p. 22.

16 R. T. France, *Divine Government*, London: SPCK, 1990, p. 22.

17 George Eldon Ladd, *The Presence of the Future*, London: SPCK, 1974.

18 David Bosch, 'Evangelism and Social Transformation', in Tom Sine (ed.), *The Church in Response to Human Need*, Monrovia: Marc, 1983, p. 277f.

19 Jeremias, *New Testament Theology*, p. 101.

20 Tom Wright, *Paul for Everyone – Ephesians*, London: SPCK, 2002, p. 12.

21 William Dyrness, *The Earth Is God's*, New York: Orbis, 1997, p. 15.

22 This is a major part of the letter to the Hebrews.

23 Douglas Farrow, *Ascension and Ecclesia*, Edinburgh: T. & T. Clark, 1999.

24 David Runcorn, *Choice Desire and the Will of God*, London: SPCK, 2003.

25 Dyrness, *The Earth Is God's*, p. xiv.

26 See Col. 1:20.

27 See Gen. 1:27–30.

28 Tom Smail, *Once and for All*, London: Darton, Longman and Todd, 1998.

29 Miroslav Volf, *Exclusion and Embrace*, Oxford: Abingdon, 1996, p. 126.

13 The presence of the future

This truth gives us our direction and sense of belonging in life

This section has touched on each of the key parts of the great story of our salvation, from creation and fall, to Christ's incarnation, death, resurrection and ascension, all culminating in Christ's return and the transformation of heaven and earth.

> The Christian metanarrative (great story) is the biblical story of the world from creation to consummation. It is the story of the trinitarian God's relationship with his creation. It sees God as the beginning and end of all things, their source and their goal, Creator and Lord, Redeemer and Renewer, the one who was and who is and who is to come. It is a story which is not yet completed ... The end of the story is still to come, with the God who is also to come to his creation in the end.[1]

The church's identity and mission are determined by its place in this story. We participate in the critical act between Christ's ascension and return. If we know that the eternal life we have in Christ includes a transformed world, rather than escapes from the world and the whole physical dimension of life, we will treat the earth and human society differently. 'This means that those who live by this story live within it. It gives us our identity, our place in the story, and a part to play in the still-to-be-completed purposes of God for his world.'[2]

It is not just that knowing the destination shapes the journey. If the kingdom of God has been having an impact on the world since Jesus came, then we can expect to have a part to play in its ministry now. Commitment to the transformation of the world, the transformation of communities, is inherent within Christian discipleship. We are either Christian citizens and public disciples, or we are doubly unworthy servants!

Two biblical guarantees about the future

How can we be sure that this is God's purpose for us and for the world? The Bible offers two guarantees. One is a fact of history, the other a personal encounter. In each case Paul uses a harvest festival expression, 'first fruits'. In the Old Testament era, the Israelites celebrated two harvest festivals. The primary one, when 'all was safely gathered in', was called Tabernacles or Booths. It lasted a week and was a great celebration and thanksgiving for that year's harvest. Interestingly, it was a celebration of redemption and the Redeemer, as much as of harvest and the Creator. The booths were simple shelters which people built and camped in for the whole week. Each year it acted as a living reminder that they were only in their 'land flowing with milk and honey' because their God had brought them out of Egypt and kept their nation alive through forty years in the wilderness, where they lived in tents. It was a reminder that it is not possible to separate creation from redemption. They were tempted to forget their Redeemer now that they were settled in the promised land. We are tempted to forget the creation and our responsibility to the human community, and treat redemption as an escape. The technical term for the theology of Christian hope and the last, or ultimate, things is 'eschatology'. The temptation is to treat it as escapology!

But to return to harvest festivals, the Israelites had another, shorter, festival right at the beginning of the harvest season, fifty days after Passover. It was called 'first fruits', or Pentecost (because of the fifty days). It later came to be associated with the giving of the law, but its essence was the start of the harvest. Imagine a corner of a field or greenhouse which the sun regularly reaches first and where the tomatoes – or grapes, or wheat, or whatever the crop might be – ripen ahead of the rest. That is first fruits. It is the first part of the harvest. It is of exactly the same kind as the rest of the harvest, but it has arrived early. It provides a literal foretaste of the complete harvest, which is still to come. It also acts as a kind of promise or guarantee that final harvest time is in sight and will arrive. The Israelites offered those first fruits to God in thanksgiving and faith.

Paul applies this first to Christ and then to us.

1. The resurrection

Paul says that Christ's resurrection is the first fruits of the resurrection of all who 'belong' to Christ. As he was raised from the dead, never to die again, so it will be for them, for all believers.

> If for this life only we have hoped in Christ, we are of all people most to be pitied.
>
> But in fact Christ has been raised from the dead, the first fruits of those who have died. For since death came through a human being, the resurrection of the dead has also come through a human being; for as all die in Adam, so all will be made alive in Christ. But each in his own order: Christ the first fruits, then at his coming those who belong to Christ.
>
> (1 Cor. 15:19–23)

What God did to Jesus, raising him from the dead as the turning point of history, he will do for all who believe, at the climax of history. The Bible also teaches that there will be a general resurrection in anticipation of the final judgment.[3] But in 1 Corinthians 15, Paul is focusing on the nature of the believers' final hope. Just as, in Revelation, the passage about the new heaven and earth follows the passage about general resurrection and final judgment, so Paul is primarily concerned about the risen life which follows, once death is no more.

Then comes the end, when he hands over the kingdom to God the Father, after he has destroyed every ruler and every authority and power. For he must reign until he has put all his enemies under his feet. The last enemy to be destroyed is death. For 'God has put all things in subjection under his feet.' But when it says, 'All things are put in subjection,' it is plain that this does not include the one who put all things in subjection under him. When all things are subjected to him, then the Son himself will also be subjected to the one who put all things in subjection under him, so that God may be all in all.

(1 Cor. 15:24–28)

Christ's physical resurrection not only guarantees our resurrection, but is also the prototype of it. Based on what happened to Christ, Paul outlines the continuities and the discontinuities between our present physical state, which is perishable, and our future one, which is imperishable. 'Just as we have borne the image of the man of dust, we will also bear the image of the man of heaven' (1 Cor. 15:49). In 2 Corinthians he even speaks of a new body being kept in heaven for us. Our present body is like a tent, but the new one is like a house. The mortal will be swallowed up by life.[4]

For Paul, the resurrection of Jesus is the beginning of the new creation. In parallel with Jesus' language about the kingdom of God, the new creation is already and not yet, the beginning of the future in the present. This is not surprising, as 'the kingdom of God is creation healed'.[5]

Just as we see Jesus' resurrection as the origin and guarantee of human hope, so we can see it as the origin and guarantee of a universal hope. The significance of the empty tomb is that the Lord's risen and glorified body is the transmuted form of his dead body. Thus matter itself participates in the resurrection transformation, enjoying thereby the foretaste of its own redemption from decay. The resurrection of Jesus is the seminal event from which the whole of God's new creation has already begun to grow.[6]

Paul is never particularly interested in esoteric teaching about the future, which has no practical outcome. His teaching always has a here-and-now application. So in 1 Corinthians he urges, 'Therefore, my beloved, be steadfast, immovable, always excelling in the work of the Lord, because you know that in the Lord your labour is not in vain' (1 Cor. 15:58). In other words, the fact of Christ's resurrection, and the new creation which it initiates, is the guarantee of our resurrection. And the work we do before the great day of resurrection is not wasted; it will have a place in God's renewed world. Christian citizenship is worthwhile. Distinctive involvement and subversive engagement can make an eternal contribution. Christian disciples have the privilege of doing things that can last for ever.

> To be a Christian might be defined as living in the light cast by the resurrection; living, that is to say, as those who insist on interpreting this world in terms of its (surprising and unexpected) future as made known to us in the resurrection of Jesus by his Father in the power of the Holy Spirit.[7]

Personal conversion is entry into the new creation. 'So if anyone is in Christ, there is a new creation: everything old has passed away; see, everything has become new!' (2 Cor. 5:17) Paul is saying that individual believers are part of the new creation, but his primary point is that the fact that people are in Christ is evidence that the new creation has already begun. Conversion is essential in more ways than one. It is essential for salvation, but it is also recruitment for its ministry here and now. It changes the way we see our fellow humans.

> For the love of Christ urges us on, because we are convinced that one has died for all; therefore all have died. And he died for all, so that those who live might live no longer for themselves, but for him who died and was raised for them.
>
> From now on, therefore, we regard no one from a human point of view; even though we once knew Christ from a human point of view, we know him no longer in that way.
>
> (2 Cor. 5:14–16)

Clark Pinnock comments, 'Conversion points not only to individual change but beyond to the coming transformation of the world. Since we are creatures in society and in the world, God wants to renew both us and our created context.'[8]

The first guarantee from God is the resurrection of his Son. The resurrection guarantees God's enduring commitment to his creation, and is itself the beginning of the new creation.

2. The Holy Spirit

The resurrection as the first fruit happened to Jesus, and guarantees that a similar resurrection will one day happen to us also. The other first fruit happened to Jesus and happens to us in this life. It is the gift of the Holy Spirit. Every Christian is indwelled by the Holy Spirit. But we are expected to understand what this gift is for.

There is a direct connection between the two first fruits. The Father raised his Son by the power of the Holy Spirit. As a consequence of Christ's death and resurrection, that same Holy Spirit lives in us. 'If the Spirit of him who raised Jesus from the dead dwells in you, he who raised Christ from the dead will give life to your mortal bodies also through his Spirit that dwells in you' (Rom. 8:11). Paul refers to the Holy Spirit as first fruits in the passage about the new creation which we considered earlier. 'And not only the creation, but we ourselves, who have the first fruits of the Spirit, groan inwardly while we wait for adoption, the redemption of our bodies' (Rom. 8:23). This was a natural connection for him to make. After all, the feast of first fruits is also called Pentecost and was the day when the Holy Spirit was first poured out upon the church.

But 'first fruits' implies that a second stage is awaited.

> In the New Testament era there are two main stages in the fulfilment of the promise of the Holy Spirit. The first stage is realized in the outpouring of the Spirit at Pentecost. This is the gift of 'first fruits' in Rom. 8:23 and of the guarantee in 2 Cor. 1:22, 5:5 and Eph. 1:14. The second stage is the coming of the Messiah with the resurrection of the dead and the establishment of the new heaven and the new earth, both totally the work of the Holy Spirit. Only at this stage will the limitations, constraints and frustrations of the present age be removed.[9]

The Holy Spirit is given for a double purpose. He is the source of assurance, giving believers evidence that they are indeed Christ's and that they have a place in the future kingdom. The Spirit is 'the certain evidence that the future had dawned, and the absolute guarantee of its final consummation'.[10] But at the same time, the Spirit empowers Christians to live the life of the future in advance. His presence and power gives focus and practical purpose to our discipleship. 'By the Spirit's presence believers tasted of the life to come and became oriented towards its consummation.'[11] There is a dynamic in the Spirit's work in us. The 'already' of the kingdom means that there is fruitful work possible now. The 'not yet' motivates us to push on, while always longing for the final coming of the King. 'The presence of the Holy Spirit ... stirs up the desire and yearning for the coming kingdom and the full rule of the king. The Spirit of God is always pushing towards the completion of all things.'[12]

Human beings do not 'build' the kingdom of God. It is not a matter of human ability or success. The kingdom is God acting as king. But God works in and through his people. The Spirit is his 'empowering presence'. 'The Holy Spirit brings forward a reality which is grounded in divine promise rather than in human thought or achievement.'[13] The power which, one day, will transform the universe is present now, in the church. Christian citizenship is only Christian when it is in the power of the Holy Spirit.

> What do we mean by [experiences of the Holy Spirit]? We are saying that these experiences are of unfathomable depth, because in them God himself is present in us, so that in the immanence of our hearts we discover a transcendent depth. If this Spirit of God is 'the Spirit of the resurrection', then we are possessed by a hope which sees unlimited possibilities ahead, because it looks to God's future. The heart expands. The goals of hope in our own lives, and what we ourselves expect of life, fuse with God's promises for a new creation of all things. This gives our own finite and limited life an infinite meaning.[14]

If only we can grasp the implications of this and get away from the idea that the Spirit is just there for our personal assurance, witness and growth in grace (though he is there for those things), then we will begin to engage with our society as God intends.

No wonder that both Old and New Testaments connect the work of the Spirit with dreams and visions.[15] The Eden projects in Greater

Manchester came out of a vision given by the Holy Spirit, which was then tested out by church leaders. The resulting work is seeing significant changes both in lives and communities. It is not a quick fix, nor has it led to all the changes the teams would love to see, but it is evidence of the work of the Holy Spirit. In fact, the teams' capacity to stay and remain true to their vision long term is as much an evidence of the work of the Spirit as the changes and conversions which have taken place.

God's agents for change

Christians are God's agents for change. In this they aim to share what they have found. They have discovered the grace of God and his capacity to change them for the better. The past cannot hold them completely captive. As a Church of England report said, 'I am determined by the future God has promised rather than by the past I have made.'[16] To share in the Holy Spirit is to taste 'the powers of the age to come'. Once we have had that taste, we cannot remain satisfied with the way in which the present age, the world, is panning out. Nor can we withdraw and sit out the time until Jesus returns. The Spirit of God is at work in the world, through the church. His ministry provides a foretaste of what the world will one day be, and he equips us to take part in this ministry.

The Spirit equips the church with a gift of godly dissatisfaction. However much we see God do, given the state of the world, we can never be satisfied. One of the consequences of all that we see God 'already' doing is an even more profound dissatisfaction with all that is 'not yet'. 'The presence of the kingdom is never such as to diminish the expectation of its future coming. Those who are aware of its presence are precisely those who pray urgently for its coming. Those who experience it are precisely those who orient their lives towards its future.'[17]

Jürgen Moltmann provides a wonderful analogy of this divine dissatisfaction, by drawing a parallel with the conversion of Paul. On the road to Damascus, Saul of Tarsus heard the risen Lord say, 'Saul, Saul, why are you persecuting me? It hurts you to kick against the goads' (Acts 26:14). The goad was the sharp stick used by an ox-driver or ploughman to stop the animal from wandering off the path. Moltmann believes that Christian faith, and the promise of the new heaven and earth, functions in the same way.

> Faith, wherever it develops into hope, causes not rest but unrest, not patience but impatience. It does not calm the unquiet heart, but is itself this unquiet heart in man. Those who hope in Christ can no longer put up with reality as it is, but begin to suffer under it, to contradict it. Peace with God means conflict with the world, for the goad of the promised future stabs inexorably into the flesh of every unfulfilled present.[18]

Christians, he says, 'can no longer put up with reality as it is'. The combination of the promise of God's future world and the experience of the Spirit motivates us to action. Nothing that will not do in God's future world can leave us satisfied now. The vision of the future kingdom is a call to action.

> Faith is not characterized by an attitude of indifference or passivity towards the way the world is ... this same call is fulfilled not by turning inwards to form some 'spiritual' community, but by immersing ourselves actively in the very midst of the world's darkness and most depraved corners as salt and light with potentially transforming impact.[19]

Colonies of heaven

One of the clearest pieces of teaching about Christian citizenship and the role of the church is found in the letter to the Philippians.

> But our citizenship is in heaven, and it is from there that we are expecting a Saviour, the Lord Jesus Christ. He will transform the body of our humiliation that it may be conformed to the body of his glory, by the power that also enables him to make all things subject to himself.
> (Phil. 3:20–21)

The letter begins with a greeting: 'Grace to you and peace from God our Father and the Lord Jesus Christ' (Phil. 1:2). In both cases, the reference is not to the Lord who is called Jesus, which would make Jesus one Lord among many. It is not just a reference to 'my Lord', but to *the Lord* of the universe, to Jesus who is the only Lord. Paul believes that the time will come when 'at the name of Jesus every knee shall bow and every tongue confess that Jesus Christ is Lord' (Phil. 2:10, alluding to Isa. 45:23). If he is Lord of all, this cannot be a private matter. His citizens will be expected to obey him and to serve him in all of life, not just in private. Recent scholarship has demonstrated that in Philippians, Paul is not only insisting on the lordship of Christ, but is deliberately contrasting Christ's way of being Lord with Caesar's.[20] 'Paul's gospel was a royal proclamation aimed at challenging other royal proclamations . . . Caesar demanded worship as well as "secular" obedience, not just taxes but sacrifices. He was well on the way to becoming the supreme divinity in the Greco-Roman world.'[21]

This sort of public discipleship can be costly. Paul is writing from Caesar's prison, but God is using the imprisonment for his kingdom.

> It is right for me to think this way about all of you, because you hold me in your heart, for all of you share in God's grace with me, both in my imprisonment and in the defence and confirmation of the gospel . . .
>
> I want you to know, beloved, that what has happened to me has actually helped to spread the gospel, so that it has become known throughout the whole imperial guard and to everyone else that my imprisonment is for Christ; and most of the brothers and sisters, having been made confident in the Lord by my imprisonment, dare to speak the word with greater boldness and without fear.
> (Phil. 1:7, 12–14)

Paul spells out the way this potentially costly discipleship is to look. Philippi was a Roman colony. It had been founded by the Emperor Augustus, when he won the civil war which followed the assassination of Julius Caesar. Rather than punish his rivals' soldiers, he resettled many of them in colonies, including Philippi. Citizens of colonies were also citizens of Rome, but they were not expected to return to live in the capital. They were to be a permanent presence where they had been located. Their job was to Romanize the area which had been colonized: to make it a 'Rome away from Rome'. If the local population resisted, then the emperor would come from Rome with his legions and put down the resistance.

Paul uses this as an analogy for Christian citizenship, with the very important difference that Jesus the Lord gained his authority by self-giving love and the sacrifice of himself. The Philippian church derived its citizenship from heaven, just as the retired soldiers derived theirs from Rome. Like the Roman colonists, the church was there for a purpose, to have an impact on the whole area with the values of the kingdom of God. This might prove to be a very costly way of life, especially as violence and coercion have no place in God's kingdom. But the church lived by a promise different from the one given by the emperor. The emperor would come only if the colony was in serious trouble. The Lord Jesus had promised to come at the climax of the age. The church was not living on earth until it got a chance to leave earth behind and go to heaven. It was preparing the way of the Lord and doing what it could to hasten his coming.[22]

When that would happen was unknown. That it would happen was certain. The shape of that future was also certain: 'He will transform the body of our humiliation that it may be conformed to the body of his glory, by the power that also enables him to make all things subject to himself' (Phil. 3:21).

Everything would be submitted to Jesus. The believers' bodies would be transformed to be like his risen body. Christian citizenship is to live publicly in such a way that we prepare the way for the Lord.

So Paul tells them not to give up. 'Therefore, my brothers and sisters, whom I love and long for, my joy and crown, stand firm in the Lord in this way, my beloved' (Phil. 4:1).

The justified act justly and seek justice

The letter to Philippi connects us to another important theme: the relationship between discipleship and justice. Paul lists a wonderful group of qualities, which public disciples are to focus on and put into action.

Finally, beloved, whatever is true, whatever is honourable, whatever
is just, whatever is pure, whatever is pleasing, whatever is
commendable, if there is any excellence and if there is anything
worthy of praise, think about these things. Keep on doing the things
that you have learned and received and heard and seen in me, and
the God of peace will be with you.
(Phil. 4:8–9)

One of these themes is justice: 'whatever is just'. Those who are
justified through the cross must act justly. This is a connection which
has often been overlooked. The theological disputes between Roman
Catholics and Protestants have resulted in Bible translations with
different emphases. Catholic Bibles tend to have the word 'justice'
where Protestant translations have 'righteousness'. Leaving aside the
reasons for the difference, the consequence is that Protestant or
evangelical Christians often miss the connection, in New Testament
Greek, between justice and justification. In fact, both words have their
roots in the Old Testament and are usually found together. A well-
known example is found in Amos 5:24: 'But let justice roll down like
waters, and righteousness like an ever-flowing stream.'

Righteousness and justice form one integrated quality. Hebrew
thought never imagined theoretical concepts, but was concerned
with actual behaviour. God's Old Testament people were to act
justly because they were a redeemed people whom God had set free
from injustice.

When Paul teaches about justification, he makes it clear that the
cross, through which we are justified and have peace with God, is an
event where God demonstrates that he is just.

For there is no distinction, since all have sinned and fall short of the
glory of God; they are now justified by his grace as a gift, through the
redemption that is in Christ Jesus, whom God put forward as a
sacrifice of atonement by his blood, effective through faith. He did
this to show his righteousness, because in his divine forbearance he
had passed over the sins previously committed; it was to prove at the
present time that he himself is righteous [just!] and that he justifies
the one who has faith in Jesus.
(Rom. 3:23–26)

Salvation in Old and New Testaments involves God acting justly. Conversion is recruitment for the cause of divine justice. If we take a brief look at the teaching of Jesus, once we understand that righteousness involves justice, the seeking of justice becomes central to Christian discipleship. In the Sermon on the Mount, the blessing on the meek, that they will inherit the earth (very strange if the earth has no future), is immediately followed by the statement, 'Blessed are those who hunger and thirst for righteousness/justice, for they will be filled.' Later Jesus says, 'Strive first for the kingdom of God and his righteousness/justice, and all these things will be given to you as well.' The Bible does not split our inner qualities like righteousness (as we have often interpreted it) from our actions like justice. The Old Testament Christians had to ensure justice for aliens because they had been aliens, unjustly treated in Egypt. To seek justice for all, 'whatever is just', is a core component of public discipleship.

Restored stewards of the earth

Paul teaches that those who have received God's grace and been justified 'will exercise dominion in life through the one man, Jesus Christ' (Rom. 5:17). This is a direct reference to Genesis 1 – 3. The human race is created in their Creator's image. This means that humans are sufficiently like God to be able to have a relationship with him. Created in the image of the triune God, we have the capacity to relate to one another and form community. Together as a race, we are commissioned to construct culture and to be the stewards of the earth. But we are a fallen race who have abused the stewardship which was granted us. We are made in God's image to partner him in his activity, but we have treated the earth as though it were our own and we could do what we liked with it.

In Christ, that stewardship of the earth is restored. There is nothing so green as evangelism, properly understood. What we are restored to is an active partnership with God. 'We do God's will ... by working alongside God in bringing people and the earth to the place where they reflect the divine glory.'[23] We are his apprentices. His hands are already upon everything that our hands touch. His mind already sustains everything that our minds address. (Science really is 'thinking God's thoughts after him'.) 'We are called to reflect God's own commitment to the world.'[24]

Faithfulness and discernment

Whether it be environmental concern, the struggle for justice, or the transformation of a city, I hope it is now clear that all Christians are called to public discipleship, to citizenship of Christ's kingdom for the benefit of all, because that is what Christ came for. We do not live this way because we are guaranteed success. The history of the church contains wonderful stories of transformation, and as many times when transformation was resisted and the church could only live as a faithful alternative society. 'God has broken into history – the new age has begun. We wait for the consummation of history and hope for the glory of God. We are neither optimistic nor pessimistic about the world, but wait in hope, serving the Lord.'[25] We live this way because it is right. There is no room for triumphalism or fatalism. What is required is faith, faithfulness and, above all, discernment.

Christians should always be willing to stand up and be counted when, on the basis of our faith, there is a clear issue of right and wrong. It is vital that we do this, because increasingly our fellow citizens find it difficult to provide a moral justification for things they often still feel are right and wrong. All people have a conscience. All are made in God's image. And the Christian faith has had an impact on and shaped this nation for centuries. Many of the things people appreciate about our society are the fruit of the Christian faith. They have been grown on the Christian tree. But these days their connection to Christianity is not obvious. So we need to take a stand, not just for our own rights as citizens who are Christians, but on all matters concerning justice, the environment, sustaining the family, and so on. This sort of grass-roots pressure through writing to an MP, joining an e-mail campaign, buying Fair Trade goods, and so on, should be a normal part of Christian discipleship, and is politically important. Grass-roots pressure really can bring political change. The Jubilee 2000 campaign about poor countries' debt originated in and was heavily supported by the churches, working with all sorts of people and organizations sharing this concern. There was common ground, just as Paul found in Corinth. Make Poverty History, which had an even bigger alliance, was its natural successor. The island of Madagascar, whose Anglican church is twinned with the diocese in which I serve, has had its debt cleared because of that grass-roots pressure. Public discipleship works.

Christian citizens should always stand up and be counted when there is a clear issue of right and wrong. But some issues are not that clear and we should always check our facts, talk with other Christians, and not react to the first appeal we receive or news item we see. Discernment is necessary.

It is also necessary when deciding which initiatives to take locally. Jesus described his ministry as seeing and hearing what the Father was doing (John 5:19). As his disciples, we are called to do the same: 'Humbly watching in any situation in which we find ourselves in order to learn what God is trying to do there, and then doing it with him.'[26] This sort of discernment is birthed in prayer. Churches that keep informed about their communities and pray regularly for them are much more likely to discern correctly.

It is necessary because there are so many things with which a church or group of churches could get involved, that it would not be possible or wise to try them all. The basis for discernment and action is always the question, 'Can this become something that can belong in the coming age?' But discernment is also about being in step with God's timing. God is always ahead of us in mission. Sometimes discernment involves discerning God's action in our communities. Sometimes he will take something we are doing and make of it more than we could have imagined.

> It is a vital part of a Christian perspective on this world to identify within it scattered acts of recreative anticipation of God's promised future, as the same Spirit who raised Jesus from death calls into being life, health, faith and hope where there is otherwise no capacity for these and no accounting for them. Such anticipations are to be found in this world, but they are not of this world.[27]

Such events happen because of the Holy Spirit. If the Spirit is the foretaste of the power of the new heaven and earth, we should, at times, see him act in a way that really is an imperfect foretaste of the future world.

One example in my experience came when the Soul Survivor youth ministry was involved in The Message, a holistic mission (mentioned previously) in the estates of Greater Manchester. We were partnered by British Youth for Christ, the Oasis Trust and the Message Trust, who had begun their Eden programme a few years earlier. Ten thousand Christian young people took part in one of two five-day missions. The whole venture had the support of 200 local churches and was sustained in prayer by the Manchester Prayer Network.

There are many stories to tell from that week,[28] but I want to focus on one, the Open Valley project in Swinton. The Greater Manchester Police Community Development Department had directed us to the Valley Estate. The estate was trapped between two trunk roads. There was one road in and one out. (It reminded me of a South African township from apartheid days.) The roads on the estate were blocked with concrete bollards, because car crime, along with burglary and violence, was endemic. Many houses (I was told one in four) were closed up with metal shutters. Those gardens had anything up to ten years' worth of rubbish dumped in them. The connecting path between the two halves of the estate was over-grown with shrubbery. It was hardly ever used, because it backed on to the local drug dealer's house and was not considered safe. The whole area was overgrown and there was a horrible atmosphere of neglect. But there was a residents' association desperate for change and talking to the police. (The Holy Spirit was working there ahead of us.)

We arranged for teams of up to 750 young people to work on the estate for each afternoon of the mission. Over eight afternoons, they cleared 280 tonnes of rubbish by hand and they tidied up 200 gardens. They cleared an area for an adventure playground, a park and a dog-walking area. They cleaned streets, they cleaned up the run-down community centre and did the (unskilled) work to prepare a house to be a community resource centre. The police and local authority succeeded in evicting the drug dealer, allowing our teams to clear the connecting path. The *Manchester Evening News* headline said, 'Who needs Charlie [Dimmock]? We've got our own Ground Force here.'

As the word got out, people started to offer help. When we got to the replanting stage for the park, I remember police Land Rovers coming in, full of plants donated by local garden centres. One local businessman heard about the connecting path and provided the tarmac so that the improvement could be permanent. Each of our teams included a member of the local community, to ensure that we did only what the residents wanted. Many residents joined in. The local ladies' group spent their bingo night money on ice creams for the team. I will always remember the little boy, living with his Gran, who watched out for the coaches each afternoon and then ran down the street shouting, 'The Christians are coming! The Christians are coming!'

A number of people from the estate also became Christians that week, although we were trying hard to witness through deeds rather than words. (There were evening evangelistic youth events in the city centre.) One man told me that he had met his neighbour at the end of his garden for the first time. A group of young people from Colorado spent their 'holiday' in England clearing the badly overgrown garden. The neighbours were celebrating with a barbecue that weekend. Two streets, which had been at war with one another, were reconciled and worked together on the projects. Most remarkably, there was no recorded crime for the duration of the mission. I heard that personally from the community policeman. And he went public. At the final evening rally, he stood on stage and said, 'Question: How do you get a zero rate of crime for ten days on one of the country's roughest housing estates? Answer: Bring in 1,000 Christian youngsters.' Even more importantly, the crime rate on the estate fell by 46% and stayed down in the years that followed. A church was planted on the estate,[29] and the local schools continue to be visited by The Tribe, the Message to Schools band. The Message Trust is now a partner in the Greater Manchester Police's annual crime prevention awards.

When Soul Survivor began to plan Soul in the City,[30] a similar event in London for 2004, the Chief Constable of Greater Manchester wrote to the Commissioner of the Metropolitan Police to commend us. As a result, the Met became a major active supporter of Soul in the City.

God was there ahead of us. The Tribe were known to all the estate kids because they regularly visited their schools. The residents' association was desperate for change. The key police officer in the Community Development Department turned out to be an active Christian. Most of what happened was not achieved by the young people. Their very hard work was essential, but God made more of our input than it had the capacity to achieve by itself.

> Such anticipations are to be found in this world, but they are not of this world. They belong to God's future of which they are heralds and towards which they direct our hopeful gaze. In such happenings the power of the future-made-present is manifest … Christians are called to identify and to become involved with God's Spirit in all that he is doing to fashion a genuine presence of the new within the midst of the old, drawing it into self-transcendent, albeit partial, anticipations of what will ultimately be.[31]

Notes

1 Richard Bauckham and Trevor Hart, *Hope Against Hope*, London: Darton, Longman and Todd, 1999, p. 35f.

2 Ibid.

3 See Rev. 20:11–15.

4 See 2 Cor. 5:1–4.

5 Hans Kung, *On Being a Christian*, London: Collins, 1974, quoted in Howard Snyder, *Liberating the Church*, Basingstoke: Marshall, 1983, p. 258.

6 John Polkinghorne, *The God of Hope and the End of the World*, London: SPCK, 2002, p. 113.

7 Bauckham and Hart, *Hope Against Hope*, p. 70.

8 Clark Pinnock, *Flame of Love*, Downers Grove: IVP, 1996, p. 146.

9 Peter Hocken, 'The Holy Spirit and the Coming Kingdom', in *Skepsis*, Anglican Renewal Ministries, p. 3.

10 Gordon Fee, *God's Empowering Presence*, Peabody: Hendrickson, 1994, p. 806.

11 Ibid., p. 810.

12 Hocken, 'The Holy Spirit'.

13 Church of England Doctrine Commission, *We Believe in the Holy Spirit*, London: Church House Publishing, 1991, p. 171.

14 Jürgen Moltmann, *The Spirit of Life*, London: SCM, 1992, p. 155.

15 As in Acts 2:17, quoting Joel 2:28–30.

16 Doctrine Commission, *We Believe in the Holy Spirit*, p. 173.

17 Bauckham and Hart, *Hope Against Hope*, p. 162.

18 Jürgen Moltmann, *Theology of Hope*, London: SCM, 1992, p. 21.

19 Bauckham and Hart, *Hope Against Hope*, p. 82.

20 See N. T. Wright, 'Paul's Gospel and Caesar's Empire', in Richard Horsley (ed.), *Paul and Politics*, Harrisburg: Trinity Press, 2000.

21 Ibid., p. 168.

22 See 2 Pet. 3:12, 'waiting for and hastening the coming of the day of God'.

23 William Dyrness, *The Earth Is God's*, New York: Orbis, 1997, p. 58.

24 Ibid., p. 69.

25 Pinnock, *Flame of Love*, p. 147.

26 John V. Taylor, *The Go Between God*, London: SCM, 1972, p. 39.

27 Bauckham and Hart, *Hope Against Hope*, p. 70f.

28 See *The Urban Adventure – Soul Survivor Message 2000*, Soul Survivor, 2005.

29 See George Lings, 'The Eden Puzzle', *Encounters on the Edge*, 14, Church Army, May 2002.

30 See *Urban Legends – Soul in the City 2004*, Soul Survivor, 2005.

31 Bauckham and Hart, *Hope Against Hope*, p. 70f.

14 The way of Jesus

Earlier in this book, we saw what public discipleship looked like for the Corinthian Christians. Paul called them to follow his example to the extent that he was imitating Christ (1 Cor. 11:1). Public discipleship must be an imitation of Christ in the power of the Spirit. Jesus Christ is our ultimate model for ministry. 'Any doctrine of the incarnation and any concern to root Christian faith in history must regard the ministry of Jesus on earth as a matter of supreme interest and significance.'[1] His ministry in the Gospels should be a primary source, as we discern the shape of Christian citizenship.

As we saw in Section Three, Jesus refused to separate love of God from love of neighbour. Enquiries about *the* great commandment were always answered with the two.[2] This is not a split or dual loyalty, but the way God intends his people to live on earth. We cannot serve God without serving our fellow human beings. When there is a clash of loyalties, Jesus' example before Herod, the high priest and Pilate makes it clear that loyalty to God must come first. But even when Jesus was on trial before Pilate, he acknowledged that Pilate's authority (which Pilate was abusing) came from the Father in heaven.[3] The state is not a separate realm. Human authority and leadership have an appropriate place within God's kingdom. But public leaders are also called to a servant authority and leadership as modelled by Christ.

Jesus lived out his calling from the Father by identification, compassion, teaching, action and the forming of a community.

Identification

As we have seen, the incarnation, when the Word became flesh, is the great identification of God with the human race. It is a permanent identification. That flesh has never been laid aside, just transformed through death and resurrection. 'The incarnation, and Christ's work flowing out of it ... was an act of profound affinity, a radical identification with all that it means to be human.'[4] But Jesus also identified himself with us in his baptism, much to the perplexity of his cousin John the Baptist.[5] In his baptism he identified with the reality of our sin and impending judgment. The baptism is the first anticipation of the cross in his adult ministry. That profound identification is characteristic of his ministry from then on. He never romanticizes sin and evil, or pretends that it does not matter, whether in high or low.[6] But he is never condemning and never writes people off, although he gives dire warnings on occasions. He is toughest on people who believe that others are excluded from the kingdom, by their ignorance or their sin, while they themselves are 'not as others'.

Christian citizenship requires that same identification. Unlike their Lord, Christian citizens are not 'without sin', so they should not find it difficult to identify with fellow sinners, but do need to heed Jesus' warnings. This costly identification with others and commitment to them puts the 'involved' into involved distinctiveness and the 'engagement' into subversive engagement. Jesus' utter loyalty to the Father, set above all other loyalties, puts the 'distinctiveness' and 'subversion' into the mix.

Compassion

Jesus' identification with the people is demonstrated in his profound compassion. His response to the plight of the blind, of lepers, of a hungry crowd with nothing to eat, or of a bereaved mother, is to be moved with pity or compassion. He responds in the same way to complete strangers as he does to his friends Mary and Martha in their loss of Lazarus.[7] 'When he saw the crowds, he had compassion for them, because they were harassed and helpless, like sheep without a shepherd' (Matt. 9:26). But Christ's compassion was not a general feeling sorry for people. His love and commitment were total, but it was also based on a clear, objective discernment of their need. 'Sheep without a shepherd' was not a farming analogy. It was an Old Testament image for Israel and the failure of its leaders.[8] This nation needed its true king. Their profound physical, social and political needs were deeply rooted in their spiritual needs. Jesus engaged with them on every level.

His compassion was both distinctive and subversive. He upheld the highest standards of human behaviour, and applied the law to the intentions and motivations of our hearts, as well as to our actions. 'Be perfect therefore, as your heavenly Father is perfect' (Matt. 5:48). But he met people with forgiveness and grace rather than judgment. The men who wanted to stone a woman taken in adultery were told to examine their own hearts and motives first, and then cast their stones. The whole ministry of Christ on earth could be summed up as 'embodied holy compassion'. This unusual combination of the highest moral standards and the deepest love and concern is the distinctive quality of Christian citizenship.

Teaching

Much of Jesus' teaching was to the crowds. He also taught his disciples in private, but his central teaching about the kingdom of God was intended for a wider audience. As 'your kingdom come' meant 'your will be done on earth as it is in heaven', there is and was scope for application to every aspect of life. In the same way, it is a Christian responsibility to 'teach' our society the ways of Christ. Apart from on church platforms, this will mainly be done by engaging in informed public debate, from a distinctive Christian viewpoint, at all levels of society.

Near the start of his public ministry, in the synagogue at Nazareth,

Jesus read from Isaiah 61 and announced his ministry 'to bring good news to the poor ... to proclaim release to the captives and recovery of sight to the blind, to let the oppressed go free, to proclaim the year of the Lord's favour' (Luke 4:14–21; see also Isa. 61:1–2). This is often called 'the Nazareth Manifesto' and it provides a challenging template for Christian engagement with society. Isaiah 61:8 gives the biblical motivation for it all: 'for I the LORD love justice'.

The deceptively short lines which Jesus read that day contain many layers of meaning and demonstrate the breadth of Christ's concern, which we are called to share. The Old Testament words for 'poor' covered many kinds of deprivation. Preaching is only good news to the poor if it announces God's active intervention on their behalf to restore justice. To 'preach' is a word mainly used in the New Testament for evangelistic preaching. The content of this preaching was 'freedom', or release, a word applicable either to the forgiveness of sin or to release in the more physical sense. The word for 'prisoners' most commonly referred to prisoners of war. The blind who are to recover their sight clearly include the physically blind (Luke 7:21–22), but Isaiah also used the term to speak of spiritual blindness (e.g. Isa. 6:9–10). The release which is promised to the oppressed, as in the previous phrase, can speak of forgiveness or a more physical liberation. Without question, the oppressed include those who are physically, politically or economically oppressed. Jesus also released the demonically oppressed, but this word in Luke's account does not come from Isaiah 61, but rather from Isaiah 58:6, where it is found alongside the hungry, the poor wanderer without shelter, and the naked, the context being that of 'loosing the chains of injustice'. Because of the reference to 'the year of the Lord's favour', we may assume that Jesus' hearers would have understood the passage as relating to the great day of release for their people, 'the final Jubilee of history'.[9] In the Jubilee, debts were remitted, slaves were freed, and capital in the form of land was redistributed. This provides an all-embracing politics of the kingdom.

As his ministry continued, Jesus gave radical teaching about wealth and the exercise of power. He drew a direct connection between the kingdom and the command to love one's neighbour as oneself (Mark 12:28–34). But his teaching on love was extended to the alien and the enemy. He defined neighbour as the one in need whom you are able to help, even if that means crossing hostile racial barriers (Luke 10:25–27). Love of neighbour was to be extended to the love of enemies, even the occupying Roman soldier who could force you to carry his pack for a mile (Matt. 5:38–48).

Jesus was a story teller. He taught in parables. Many of the parables retold Israel's story in ways that seemed familiar when they began, but brought the listener to a conclusion they did not expect. In this way, he gave his listeners the opportunity to see their assumptions and worldview differently and to respond accordingly. The purpose of parables was 'to convey a fresh possibility to the hearer, otherwise unknown to his world or his language. As such, the parables also invite the hearer to participate in what is conveyed.'[10] God's power was as much in action in the telling of parables as in the healing of the sick. In the parables, the kingdom demands a response. They are a call to discipleship. This was subversive engagement with Israel's understanding of its story. We need to find similar, imaginative, ways to retell, subvert and challenge our nation's stories.

The parables also warn us about the danger of either distancing our understanding of the kingdom of God from public life, or equally of overidentifying any human political programme with the kingdom. The frequent introduction to parables that the kingdom of God is 'like ... ' has three clear implications. First, a kingdom that can be compared to aspects of ordinary life can be lived out in this life. Second, the frequent 'twist in the tail' of the parables shows that the kingdom is 'unlike' the way we are accustomed to live. 'The general tendency of parables is to confound our conventional and comfortable world view.'[11] Third, the kingdom may not be precisely identified with human systems, concerns or aspirations. It is 'like' rather than 'the same as'. 'There can be no one place, time, event or community which *is* the kingdom of God, anymore than *the will of God* can be tied down to any specific situation or event. The Kingdom of God is God taking control in his world.'[12]

Action

Jesus did not just teach, however. He also acted. His action gave integrity to his teaching. His sermon at Nazareth began with the reading from Isaiah, but ended with the words, 'Today this scripture has been fulfilled in your hearing' (Luke 4:21). This was early in his public ministry, but already, at least in Capernaum (see v. 23), he was doing what he claimed. Later, when John the Baptist's disciples come to him to ask, 'Are you the one who is to come, or are we to wait for another?', we hear:

> Jesus had just then cured many people of diseases, plagues, and evil spirits, and had given sight to many who were blind. And he answered them, 'Go and tell John what you have seen and heard: the blind receive their sight, the lame walk, the lepers are cleansed, the deaf hear, the dead are raised, the poor have good news brought to them. And blessed is anyone who takes no offence at me.'
> (Luke 7:20–23)

Jesus' teaching was never empty rhetoric. He did what he said.

In his ministry, the kingdom became good news to the poor at the time, not just a promise of good news in a future life. The sick were given back the possibility of an active role in society, the demonized were set free and restored to normal relationships, cleansed lepers came back into their communities. Jesus' table fellowship with tax collectors and sinners there and then was a practical foretaste of their potential place in the messianic banquet on the last day. His acceptance of women and little children gave them a special or best part in the kingdom, both present and future, which their culture did not give them. In the same way, our public discipleship will be judged much more by what we do than by what we say.

Christian citizens need to learn from Jesus. If we learn from Jesus, the poor will always be central to our concerns. They formed the great majority of his audience, and he defined his ministry in relation to them. Public discipleship will seek not only to serve the poor, but to see life from their perspective, and to address the structural injustice which keeps them poor. This has direct application to global injustice and the campaign for fair trade, but is equally applicable to Christian concern for the underclass that has developed in every Western society which has gone down the path of consumerism.

The Old Testament law and prophets had a major concern for

physical economic poverty. The Gospels continue this, but focus also on what we call social exclusion.

Jesus was committed to the breaking down of social barriers within Israel. Following his death and resurrection, the most fundamental barrier between Jew and Gentile is broken down. A study of Jesus' meal habits is particularly informative.[13]

If we are to learn from Jesus, we will view social justice as a more profound value than individual rights. We learn from Jesus that it is possible to maintain God-given moral standards within a culture of forgiveness and grace, rather than one marked by retribution and political correctness.

If we learn from Jesus, we will regard people as more important than property. We learn from Jesus the importance of forgiveness and reconciliation, of the need to go beyond violence, retaliation and enmity. South Africa's Truth and Reconcilation Commission, headed by Desmond Tutu, was a remarkable example of this being applied to public life.

If we learn from Jesus, we will work for societies which protect children, and treat them with dignity.

If we learn from Jesus, we will treat men and women as of equal status and dignity.

If we learn from Jesus, we will have the courage to challenge sin, corruption and hypocrisy in public life, wherever we find it. But we will also share his capacity to recruit the powerful for the cause of the kingdom. The remarkable work of the U2 singer Bono, which derives directly from his Christian faith, is a fine contemporary example.

If we learn from Jesus, we will maintain our public discipleship despite resistance, opposition and setbacks, trusting that it is God who brings his kingdom to its fulfilment, and who finally vindicates his servants. Above all, we learn from Jesus that short-term or provisional commitments need to be sustained by a long-term vision of the kingdom of God.

Community

Jesus' proclamation of the kingdom, demonstration of the power of the kingdom and call to discipleship resulted in the creation of a community. 'It is intended to bring about a renewed humanity.'[14] Those who, through following Jesus, recognized the absolute value of the kingdom (Matt. 13:44) and were willing to pay the price of entry (Luke 8:18–30) became closer to Jesus and to one another than any flesh-and-blood relative (Matt. 12:46–50; Luke 9:57–62). 'It was a community gathered round Jesus. Discipleship meant first and foremost following him.' But, 'Perhaps the most striking feature of all was the openness of the community of discipleship. The discipleship for which Jesus called was *both* open and committed.'[15]

Jesus continues his practical identification with the needs of men and women through his community the church, through us. One day we will all be held to account for our response to that privilege. His teaching about the sheep and the goats is not a parable. It is an analogy and a prediction.

When the Son of Man comes in his glory, and all the angels with him, then he will sit on the throne of his glory. All the nations will be gathered before him, and he will separate people one from another as a shepherd separates the sheep from the goats, and he will put the sheep at his right hand and the goats at the left. Then the king will say to those at his right hand, 'Come, you that are blessed by my Father, inherit the kingdom prepared for you from the foundation of the world; for I was hungry and you gave me food, I was thirsty and you gave me something to drink, I was a stranger and you welcomed me, I was naked and you gave me clothing, I was sick and you took care of me, I was in prison and you visited me.' Then the righteous will answer him, 'Lord, when was it that we saw you hungry and gave you food, or thirsty and gave you something to drink? And when was it that we saw you a stranger and welcomed you, or naked and gave you clothing? And when was it that we saw you sick or in prison and visited you?' And the king will answer them, 'Truly I tell you, just as you did it to one of the least of these who are members of my family, you did it to me.' Then he will say to those at his left hand, 'You that are accursed, depart from me into the eternal fire prepared for the devil and his angels; for I was hungry and you gave me no food, I was thirsty and you gave me nothing to drink, I was a stranger and you did not welcome me, naked and you did not give me clothing, sick and in prison and you did not visit me.' Then they also will answer,

'Lord, when was it that we saw you hungry or thirsty or a stranger or naked or sick or in prison, and did not take care of you?' Then he will answer them, 'Truly I tell you, just as you did not do it to one of the least of these, you did not do it to me. And these will go away into eternal punishment, but the righteous into eternal life.
(Matt. 25:31–46)

This statement of Jesus needs to be treated with great seriousness, but it should not make us underestimate the church's great tradition of service in the community and nation. Tony Blair recently told a gathering of church leaders, 'The voluntary sector, including the churches and faith communities, have always played a significant role in social action in Britain – in education, in welfare, in support for so many of the most vulnerable and needy in our society. Virtually every community in the country benefits from your work in some way.'[16] There is no room for complacency, but considerable room for gratitude to God.

Count the cost

Discipleship is a lifelong status for Christian believers. In the Gospels the disciples were continually caught out and disconcerted by Jesus' teaching. Rather than alarm us, this should give us hope. If the disciples were continually discomfited, however, the religious and political leaders were the most threatened. As the proclamation and ministry of the kingdom of God could provoke vehement opposition, then self-evidently the kingdom had not reached its consummation. Jesus used future language as well as present language (e.g. Matt. 20:1–16; 22:1–14; 24; 25).[17] The kingdom was present, but not with irresistible power. People could and did reject it. Too much happened through the ministry of Jesus to be ignored, but not enough to convince overwhelmingly. For John the Baptist, the conflict was between what Jesus was doing, the ministry of the kingdom, and the fact that he, John, was still in prison and the Gentiles had not been judged (Matt. 11:1–16). Evidently this kingdom had not finally overcome the old age, although it had powerfully assaulted it (Luke 4:31–37; 8:26–39; 10:1–20; 11:21, 22; Acts 10:38).

Jesus' actions could be limited by the lack of response of others (Mark 6:1–6). His words could be misunderstood (Mark 8:1–21) or completely rejected, even by his own followers (Mark 8:31–33). The greater part of his teaching about the kingdom came in the form of parables, which some would understand and some would not (Mark 4:9–12). Likewise, Jesus' acts of power were not automatically convincing. He refused to respond to those who demanded overwhelming proof (Luke 11:16, 29–32). His deliverance ministry could be interpreted as being of demonic origin (Luke 11:14, 15), and his table fellowship with the disreputable as a contradiction of his claims to divine inspiration (Luke 7:36–39). Jesus did not encourage his public reputation as a 'miracle worker' (e.g. Mark 2:43–45). His primary concern was for the well-being of those he healed or set free, yet his deeds were signs of the kingdom, in that they were genuine experiences of the transforming power or transformed relationships of the kingdom, which pointed beyond themselves to the future consummated kingdom and presented a challenge to faith in the present.

If we are to learn from Jesus at all, we have to learn that public discipleship can be costly. Because of the conflict between this age (and those who want it to stay the way it is) and the next, there is a risk of conflict and a potential for suffering in all public discipleship.

'The Son of Man must undergo great suffering, and be rejected by the elders, chief priests, and scribes, and be killed, and on the third day be raised.'

Then he said to them all, 'If any want to become my followers, let them deny themselves and take up their cross daily and follow me. For those who want to save their life will lose it, and those who lose their life for my sake will save it. What does it profit them if they gain the whole world, but lose or forfeit themselves? Those who are ashamed of me and of my words, of them the Son of Man will be ashamed when he comes in his glory and the glory of the Father and of the holy angels.'

(Luke 9:22–26)

Many fine Christian leaders, including Martin Luther King, Janani Luwum and Oscar Romero, have proved the truth of these words.

Christian citizenship carries no guarantee of public 'success'. It can also be a path to suffering.

Our culture avoids suffering at any cost. Suffering, however, is the one aspect of the development of Christian character with which I did not engage in the third section of this book.

> Therefore, since we are justified by faith, we have peace with God through our Lord Jesus Christ, through whom we have obtained access to this grace in which we stand; and we boast in our hope of sharing the glory of God. And not only that, but we also boast in our sufferings, knowing that suffering produces endurance, and endurance produces character, and character produces hope, and hope does not disappoint us, because God's love has been poured into our hearts through the Holy Spirit that has been given to us.
> (Rom. 5:1–5)[18]

This is simply the way of Christ, and therefore the way of the public disciple.

Notes

1 James Dunn, *Jesus' Call to Discipleship*, Cambridge: Cambridge University Press, 1992, p. 122.

2 See Matt. 22:34–40; Mark 12:28–34; Luke 10:25–28.

3 See John 19:11.

4 Alan Hirsch, *The Forgotten Ways*, Grand Rapids: Brazos, 2006, p. 132.

5 See Matt. 3:13–17.

6 E.g. Luke 13:1–5.

7 See Matt. 20:34; Mark 1:41; Matt. 15:32; Luke 7; John 11:33.

8 See Num. 26:17; 1 Kgs 22:17; 2 Chr. 18:16; Zech. 12:2.

9 G. R. Beasley-Murray, *Jesus and the Kingdom of God*, Exeter: Paternoster, 1986, p. 88.

10 Bruce Chilton and J. I. H. McDonald, *Jesus and the Ethics of the Kingdom*, London: SPCK, 1987, p. 15.

11 Ibid., p. 65.

12 R. T. France, *Divine Government*, London: SPCK, 1990, p. 15.

13 See Conrad Gempf, *Mealtime Habits of the Messiah*, Grand Rapids:

Zondervan, 2005; Craig Blomberg, *Contagious Holiness*, Leicester: IVP, 2005.

14 Beasley-Murray, *Jesus and the Kingdom of God*, p. 339.

15 Dunn, *Jesus' Call to Discipleship*, pp. 111, 126.

16 Tony Blair, speech to Faithworks, 22 March 2005, see http://politics.guardian.co.uk/speeches/story/0,,1443467,00.html.

17 See Beasley-Murray, *Jesus and the Kingdom of God*, chapters 11, 12 and 14, for a discussion of the main texts.

18 See also Heb. 12:3–11; Jas 1:2–4; 1 Pet. 1:6–7.

15 Christian citizens

An active concern for the well-being of individuals, communities, nations and the environment is fundamental to Christian discipleship. Initially, it is not a matter of the distinctive vocation of some members of the church, because it is the vocation of the church as a whole. This vocation is rooted in the work of Christ in his incarnation and public ministry, in his atoning and reconciling death, in his resurrection, ascension and sending of the Spirit. It is shaped by Christian hope, by the anticipation of the new heaven and earth, which he has secured.

The church is a vital resource for communities, at every level, especially in an individualized, consumer age which corrodes character. What our society most needs, and often knows that it needs, is fundamentally undermined by many aspects of its preferred way of life. It is the cultural equivalent of my wanting to lose weight as long as I can keep eating as many fatty and sugary products as I like. We have seen that governments cannot directly generate the values which make government, and a civil society, possible. But churches do generate those values, or at least they can. 'Our major faith traditions – all of them more historic and deeply rooted than any political party or ideology – play a fundamental role in supporting and propagating values which bind us together as a nation.'[1]

The weekly business of local churches is to generate people who put God first, others second and themselves third. If this can be linked to a vision of public discipleship, it can make the most profound effect.

Christian citizenship of this sort, however, has to be authentically Christian. In earlier times, more powerfully shaped by Christendom than today's culture, a more instinctive approach, where people served their neighbours 'because it's what you do', was perhaps more acceptable and was reasonably effective. But as social capital declines, we have to be much more explicit that love of neighbour is what Christians do because they are Christians. Whether in Christendom or post-Christendom, concern is for the world as it is, our neighbours now, but always in the light of what it will be, and what they have potential to be in Christ. 'From now on, therefore, we regard no one from a human point of view; even though we once knew Christ from a human point of view, we know him no longer in that way. So if anyone is in Christ, there is a new creation: everything old has passed away; see, everything has become new!' (2 Cor. 5:16–17)

Sometimes we will have no problem agreeing with local or national concerns and agendas. We should always look for common ground if it can be found. But even common ground will be reached from a different starting point from that of those without active faith. I like Jim Wallis's metaphor of the meeting table. People gather round the table. They meet around a shared concern for their community. They come to the table from a variety of commitments to faith, or no faith. These are explicit from the beginning. No one is asserting that religion is a purely private matter, or assuming a sacred-secular split. But each party comes to offer what they can offer distinctively. Christians come to the table, overtly and unashamedly, as Christians. But the parties around the table are not defining themselves against one another, they are seeking to act together, while maintaining the integrity of each participating group.

Sometimes our Christian discernment of our communities' needs will be very different from their declared public or political priorities. This might well result in a church initiative to address a need that others do not seem to notice. Jesus' persistent reaching out to the excluded sets the example we can follow.

Sometimes we will have to stand up and say 'no', whether or not that leaves us isolated on the issue. Many Christians stand against our nation's current practice of abortion. I believe a biblical faith requires us to do so. But we should also be in the forefront of providing support for those who decide to have their babies, but do not have the personal resources to support and nurture them. Even when we have to be known for things we are *against*, it needs to be crystal clear that there is something greater that we are *for*. Above all, we are for people, real people with messy lives and difficult struggles, and we want to serve them.

I have called this positive Christian engagement 'involved distinctiveness' and 'subversive engagement'. It challenges the church to avoid every temptation to withdraw from involvement in society, apart from evangelistic raids. I must be clear that I am passionately committed to evangelism. Men and women need a Saviour, or they will never participate in the new heaven and earth. But it is easier to evangelize people whom you love and serve, who know you are committed to them as real people, than to make relationships for evangelistic purposes only.

There is a huge range of possible ways to serve. Many Christians become involved as school governors, or read with children who need extra learning support. Others participate in campaigning groups about environmental or justice issues. Part of the decline in social capital is a lack of volunteers, among a wide range of voluntary organizations which add great value to community life, or form an essential part of the safety net protecting people who are vulnerable or in need. The overcrowding of our prisons makes prison visiting a strategic involvement. Bereavement and marriage counsellors working with Cruse or Relate and similar organizations are at a premium. There is no shortage of opportunity.

Once, when I was a vicar, I worried about our church's apparent lack of involvement in social concern. We did set up a town-centre project for the homeless, providing a Sunday lunch, when the local authority centre would otherwise be closed. But when our deanery required us to gather some additional information about our congregation, I was staggered to find how many were involved in local sacrificial service without my knowing. It was immediately clear that our church's main task was to provide support for these people, and to network some who were working in similar areas. The other task which faced us was how to ensure that our small group network was a place of support for people's ministry in the workplace and the community, helping them to apply kingdom values to their daily lives. In addition, we formed a social action team of those who wanted to serve, but had no opportunity. Via social services, we were able to link our people with those in need of some support or care.

Within this whole-church commitment to public discipleship, some people will be called to specific roles of service as their primary vocation or full-time work. They may become local counsellors, MPs, charity workers, and so on. Such people should be regarded as front-line Christian workers (not full-time Christian workers – all Christians are called to that). Busy public roles may well take people away from regular fellowship. So churches should provide frameworks of support, prayer and fellowship which fit these people's timetables, rather than tell them off for not being at Bible study.

Whether Christians work professionally for the community or offer time as volunteers, whether they are involved in a church-run project or a community-based one, all need to have realistic expectations of what we can achieve. The foundational theology of this book is that God's kingdom has already broken into human history, but will not be fully established until Christ comes. The new creation has already begun among human beings, but the complete new heaven and earth comes only with him. The Holy Spirit, who will one day transform the whole created order, is present in us now, so we may hope to see provisional anticipations or signs of that future world today.

All of this means that we can expect real social transformation, but we cannot expect total transformation. From one perspective, our expectations should always be high. There is such a thing as godly dissatisfaction. But we should not withdraw because we can only bring a partial change. The MP Ann Widdicombe is well known for her Christian faith. I asked her to speak to a breakfast for leaders in public life within her constituency. The subject was religion and politics. She told us that religion was about absolute values, while politics was a pragmatic task, about achieving the possible. So her basis for voting in parliament was to decide whether each piece of legislation was a step towards God's standard for the matter, towards God's future world, or a step away. If it was a step towards, she voted in favour. If it was a step away, she voted against. Most social change is by small steps. You do not normally get a 46% reduction in crime through a ten-day youth mission. But small steps are fine, as long as we know they are steps in the right direction. It is as much an evidence of the work of the Holy Spirit when we are sustained for a long involvement, and take some small steps, as when there is a speedy or dramatic change.

The new creation has begun. Christian citizenship is about joining in. 'God is preparing for the birth of a new creation, a new heaven and a new earth ... For whatever reason the Creator invites us to participate as collaborators in birthing this new order in our lives, in our communities and in the wider world.'[2] Have you accepted his invitation?

Notes

1 Tony Blair, in a speech to the Christian Socialist Movement, 29 March 2001, see http://www.number-10.gov.uk/output/Page3243.asp.

2 Tom Sine, *Wild Hope*, Speldhurst: Monarch, 1991, p. 230.

Christians and Muslims

Peter G. Riddell

This clearly argued and readable survey explores
how and why Christian–Muslim relationships can,
and urgently must, be improved.

ISBN 978-1-84474-060-4   256 page paperback   RRP £12.99

Life in our Hands

John Bryant and John Searle

John Bryant and John Searle pick a path through
the bioethical maze and explore how Christians
can make balanced ethical decisions in the current
cultural and social climate.

ISBN 978-0-85111-795-9   192 page paperback   RRP £9.99

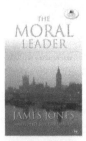

The Moral Leader

James Jones with Andrew Goddard

James Jones writes from his experience in urban
regeneration and community renewal and with the
conviction that Jesus is the model for all moral
leadership.

ISBN 978-0-85111-283-1   160 page paperback   RRP £8.99

The Incomparable Christ

John Stott

There are many ideas of Jesus, but can we know
which is the true likeness? John Stott examines the
New Testament witness to Christ, the church's
portrayal of him, and his influence on individuals.

ISBN 978-0-85111-485-9   224 page paperback   RRP £9.99

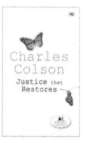

Justice that Restores

Charles Colson

Colson contends that by returning to a biblical world view we can retrieve a system of justice which restores peace and order to individuals and to society.

ISBN 978-0-85111-537-5   160 page paperback   RRP £8.99

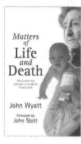

Faiths in Conflict?

Vinoth Ramachandra

This fascinating and ground-breaking study examines the complex interaction of four major world faiths.

ISBN 978-0-85111-650-1   192 page paperback   RRP £8.99

Matters of Life and Death

John Wyatt

Professor Wyatt explores the issues at the beginning and end of life from his experience as a medical practitioner.

ISBN 978-0-85111-588-7   256 page paperback   RRP £9.99

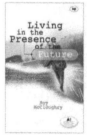

Living in the Presence of the Future

Roy McCloughry

Should we live for today; let the future take care of itself? Is everything just chance? Or is the future full of possibilities if only we knew how to grasp them? Do we have a future at all?

ISBN 978-0-85111-545-0   192 page paperback   RRP £8.99